ABOUT THE AUTHOR

Bernie S. Siegel attended Cornell University Medical
College and then trained as a pediatric and general
surgeon at Yale New Haven Hospital and the children's
Hospital of Pittsburgh. In 1978 he founded ECaP
(Exceptional Cancer Patients), a form of individual and
group therapy which encourage personal change and
healing. He has written three books since 1986,
including the huge bestsellers, *Love, Medicine and Miracles*
and *Peace, Love and Healing*. Now retired as a surgeon, he
lives in Connecticut and lectures widely all over the
world.

OTHER BOOKS BY BERNIE S. SIEGEL
Love, Medicine, and Miracles
Peace, Love and Healing
How to Live Between Office Visits

Prescriptions for Living

Inspirational Lessons for a Joyful, Loving Life

BERNIE S. SIEGEL

RIDER
London   Sydney   Auckland   Johannesburg

10 9 8 7 6 5 4 3

Copyright © Bernie S. Siegal 1998

The right of Bernie S. Siegal to be identified as th4 Author of this work has been
asserted by him in accordance with the Copyright, Designs and Patents Act 1988.

First published by Harper*Collins* Publishers Inc,
10 East 53rd Street, New York, NY 10022, USA.
This edition published in 1999 by Rider,
an imprint of Ebury Press, Random House,
20 Vauxhall Bridge Road, London, SW1V 2SA
www.randomhouse.co.uk

Random House Australia (Pty) Limited
20 Alfred Street, Milsons Point, Sydney,
New South Wales 2061, Australia

Random House New Zealand Limited

18 Poland Road, Glenfield

Auckland 10, New Zealand

Random House South Africa (Pty) Limited
Endulini, 5A Jubilee Road,
Parktown, 2193, South Africa

Random House UK Limited Reg. No. 954009

Designed by Nancy Singer Olaguera

Papers used by Random House UK Limited are natural, recyclable products made
from wood grown in sustainable forests.

Printed and bound in Great Britain by Mackays of Chatham plc, Chatham, Kent

A CIP catalogue record for this book
is available from the British Library

ISBN 0-7126-7021-1

This book is dedicated to
life and the many reasons it is worth living
the sight of a newborn child
a mother's love
family
the lick of a dog & the purr of a cat
the opportunity to love and be loved
and our precious moments of shared joy and pain.

"Love is the answer. Read this book and you'll find out the question."

—BERNIE S. SIEGEL, M.D.

Contents

Acknowledgments

I want to thank George Liles for his creative assistance and Victoria Pryor and Megan Newman for being my midwives in the birthing of this book. They helped when it hurt the most.

Introduction

What Would Bernie Do Now?

ONE DAY OVER LUNCH a woman I work with told me her secret for dealing with life's difficulties. This woman does not have the kind of problem I usually write about. She does not have cancer, AIDS or multiple sclerosis. She is not living a life of doubt, guilt, blame or shame.

Quite the opposite, she is healthy and her life is a success story. She has a loving family, enjoys her work, and has risen to the top of her profession. She came to my talks and books because we work together and she'd heard my stories about how you can change your life and find peace, love and healing.

Still, she and I have learned that all people have problems, no matter how successful they appear to be. As we were talking over lunch, my friend told me that her twenty-year-old son was troubled about some decisions he had to make, and she was uncertain how to help him find solutions without meddling. She said, "I struggled with the problem for a few days, and then I used a technique I have discovered for dealing with uncertainty."

"What is that?" I asked.

"These days," she said, "when I find myself in a tough spot, I ask myself, 'Well, what would Bernie do now?'"

"So do I," I told her.

. . .

Life is difficult. We all face adversity. We all find ourselves in perplexing situations. We try things our parents and teachers taught us, and sometimes those techniques work. Other times our old methods for dealing with adversity don't work. When the problem doesn't go away or get resolved, those with an instinct for survival realize they are going to have to find new ways to respond. How can you respond in a new way? How can you change yourself?

One of the best ways to change is to act as if you are the person you want to become. When you behave as if you are a different person, you change on a very basic level—even your physiology changes. When actors and actresses perform, their body chemistry is altered by the roles they play.

You can survive tough situations and even turn them to your advantage by acting as if you are the person you want to be. When you act like that person you can become that person. The hard parts are deciding whom you want to become, being willing to rehearse until you become that person, and forgiving yourself until you do.

I have tried a number of different roles in my life all at the same time, and it doesn't work. The happiest and most sensible choice was to be one person. I decided to become a surgeon named Bernie who writes books and gives seminars to teach people what he has learned and is still learning about how to deal with life's difficulties.

ii

Transformation

BERNIE CAME INTO BEING in 1974. I was in a lot of emotional pain in those days. I was a pediatric and general surgeon at

Yale. I had a wonderful wife and five beautiful children. My life was a success by most standards, but I was unhappy because the job of being a surgeon was very painful. Like most doctors, I had been trained to view medicine as a mechanical profession and to maintain an emotional distance from sick patients and their families. I treated people's diseases and shielded myself from their lives, and I was so miserable and in so much pain behind the wall I'd built that I was considering leaving medicine. I wanted to find another career in which I would have more contact with people and could deal with my feelings and theirs.

I struggled with the loneliness and futility I felt at work. If I were a veterinarian, I'd at least be able to hug my patients. I decided that before I gave up on medicine I would try a different way of doctoring. I would allow myself to care about the patients I was caring for. Once I'd taken that step, I quickly began to see how bizarre it is to view medicine as a profession in which you stand apart from people. Yes, a surgeon deals with cancer, but these cancers are growing in *people*, and these people are facing great challenges and an enormous range of experiences and emotions. A surgeon is surrounded by people who are sick, discouraged, afraid, embittered, dying—but also courageous, loving, wise, compassionate and alive.

A doctor is in a position to help people when they need it most—to teach them, when they confront their mortality, that many of the lessons learned will be gifts, not problems. He is also in a position to learn a great deal about being human. But to learn from the people he is working with, a physician must first learn to ignore the noninvolvement credo taught in medical schools. He must begin to view patients as people rather than cases. To care about the people he is treating, and to show it. To love them, even, and to let them know that a doctor is a human being who needs love, too.

So Dr. Siegel came out from behind his desk—literally. I pushed my desk against the wall, shaved my head, and asked patients to call me by my first name. I became Bernie, and my world changed. It was now rewarding being a doctor and helping people to live.

As Bernie, I began listening to the people I was treating and learning from them—especially the ones who were dealing successfully with life-threatening illnesses. What I learned from my patients about lifestyle changes and survival behavior was so exciting to me as a doctor that I soon began sharing it with other patients. We organized a group called ECaP (Exceptional Cancer Patients), and I began giving talks and writing books about what I had learned.

The message I deliver as Bernie is not original. I learned it by listening to my patients and then by combining their wisdom with the teachings of spiritual leaders and prophets of the past. I also learned from the wisdom of more contemporary guides: in the books and letters people wrote sharing their experiences, and in spiritual stories, myths and tales.

This book is a continuation of the work I began when I became Bernie. It is a collection of stories about how to deal with life's difficulties. Most of the people in these stories have not had the great wake-up call: that is, they are not facing life-threatening illnesses. So in a sense, this book is preventive medicine. It is a prescription for living that gives you effective and healthy ways of dealing with the adversity that occurs in everyone's life. I want to help you learn to accept your mortality before something catastrophic brings you face-to-face with the end of your life.

iii
What's New?

IF I SENT THIS BOOK TO MYSELF for a comment for the book jacket, I'd write, "It's already been written. Nothing new." And I'd be correct. If you read what the great spiritual teachers of the past taught, you'll see that nothing anyone has to say today is new.

The advice to act like the person you want to become—I thought that was a clever discovery until I found out that people in Alcoholics Anonymous have been telling one another for years, "Fake it till you make it."

When I realized the importance of discovering what is within and of expressing feelings in order to heal, I wrote in my journal, "Listen to your body. It speaks the truth unless drugged. Live what your body tells you." I thought that was an exciting new insight, until I found in the gospel of St. Thomas that Christ said the same thing twenty centuries ago: "If you bring forth what is within you, what you bring forth will save you. If you do not bring forth what is within you, what you do not bring forth will destroy you."

I can give an entire medically oriented lecture on healing using quotes from the Bible as an outline. In some modern therapies, people are advised to meditate daily and to keep a journal. Centuries ago, the Kabbalah—a Jewish system of mysticism that dates from medieval times—stressed the importance of sitting quietly every day for an hour to listen and then to write what you hear. Hindu scriptures tell us that personal transformation requires action, wisdom, devotion and meditation. You learn the same lesson when you read modern descriptions of survival behaviors.

The great spiritual leaders of the past discovered everything

we need to know about dealing with adversity and living enlightened lives. The problem is, most of us are not taught these
lessons. So poor Buddha sits under a tree and becomes enlightened, and then he takes the trouble to tell people about it so they
can be enlightened, too, but how many people ever profit from
his discovery? Over the ages some followers take his teachings to
heart and become enlightened, but most of us don't seriously
listen to prophets, holy men and women. Whether we are
Buddhists, Jews, Christians, Muslims or whatever, most of us pay
minimal attention. We say, "Yes, right, I know," and then we
don't really try to understand what our spiritual leaders are trying to teach us, or even worse we end up fighting and killing one
another because of our religious differences.

Why don't we teach our children the wisdom of the ages?
We pass on the accumulated knowledge of mathematics and
science and history and literature and medicine, so why don't
we make a serious effort to pass along what people have
learned about dealing with problems and living happily? The
fact is that most of us are given only a passing introduction to
the great spiritual teaching. So we make our way through life
unenlightened. Our lives stream past while we struggle to survive. We are not even looking for enlightenment, until perhaps
we have a disaster such as cancer or AIDS and finally awaken.
Then we start to ask questions we should have been asking all
our lives: Why am I here? What do I want to do with the limited time I have left? What is required of me?

iv
Mottoes We Live and Die By

IT IS BAD ENOUGH that we are not taught how to find happiness, but for many people the situation is worse: They are actually taught how to be miserable. I was not raised this way.

I was fortunate. I was brought up by parents who knew something about love, kindness and happiness. When adversity occurred, my mother would say, "It was meant to be. God is redirecting you. Something good will come of this." When someone in the family had to make a tough decision about a job or a school, she would say, "You have a decision to make? What will make you happy?" I grew up surrounded by messages that kept me in touch with my feelings and were loving and life-enhancing. Of course, I didn't appreciate them as a kid because they seemed too philosophical and spiritual. My mother's silver-lining philosophy focused on the big picture and the long term, and I wanted short-term answers. But from experience, I came to realize her quiet confidence that our troubles would enrich us was very positive parenting. And true. Many of my redirections proved to be more valuable than my intellectual and immediate desires.

As a doctor, I was shocked to see how much people were suffering and how rare it was to have grown up with positive messages. So I started asking people at workshops to think about what they had learned—consciously or unconsciously—about life. I started asking people, "What mottoes do you live by?" Then one night a hand shot up and a woman said, "You should ask, 'What mottoes do we die by?'" So I started asking people to think about both: What did their parents teach them about living and what did they teach that might be killing them? And sadly, a lot of people have more answers to the second question than the first.

v

A Guide for the Perplexed

IT'S EASY TO BE A MONK. If you put me in a cave and bring me three meals a day, I'm going to have a wonderful life. What problems could I have? I can light a candle and read. I can light a fire and I'm warm. I don't have mail. I don't have bills. I don't have a family. The roof can't leak. I've got it easy. The only relationship I have is with the Creator. But take me out of my cave, give me a wife and five children and a nice house, then I've got problems.

That is not a complaint. I appreciate my difficulties. My problems are my teachers. Compost happens, and compost promotes growth, to put it politely. If you want to be happy, the key is learning from your problems rather than walking away from them. But how?

If we were born with an instruction book, whenever we encountered a problem our parents could say, "Look up the solution in Chapter Three!" Your book about life would tell you what to do for yourself when problems arise: when you lose an arm or develop a disease, when your girlfriend leaves you, when you aren't accepted by the college of your choice, when your parent dies, when your child dies. Whenever adversity strikes, you get out the instruction book and turn to the appropriate chapter. The problem doesn't go away magically, but your life is easier because you have a skill and strategy for dealing with the problem and learning from it.

But we aren't sent into the world with instruction manuals,

so as long as people have been writing books, they have been writing guides to living. In the twelfth century the great Jewish physician and philosopher Maimonides wrote one with the wonderful name of *The Guide of the Perplexed*. Today the front tables in the bookstores are filled with guides for the perplexed. Why are these books so popular when nothing in them is new? Because most people don't sit down and read the old books. They don't read the Bible and learn from the stories and parables, for instance, the one about the patriarch Abraham and his son Isaac. It is a powerful lesson in faith in one's Lord.

So we have to retell the story and ask, What would you answer if your Lord told you to sacrifice one of your children? What kind of parent is this? Or, What kind of lord would ask you to do this? And why?

Sometimes it helps to hear an updated parable. People who have never seen a sheep or a shepherd might not learn much from parables about lost sheep, but that same person might make sense out of a parable about satellite dishes and remote controls and television screens. So I will tell you one of God's latest parables. Perhaps you will understand it better. You are satellite dishes, remote controls and television screens. The satellite dish has the potential to receive many programs and voices. The remote control is like your mind and selects the voice you choose to listen to. The screen represents your body. That is where you manifest what the voice tells you. If you choose the wrong voice—money, power, worldly success—you will have problems manifesting a healthy, happy life. Enlightenment comes from using the remote to pick the right voice to listen to.

Asking questions is another way of refocusing our attention on spiritual matters. For example, how do you introduce yourself to God? What would you write if you were making out your own death certificate? When are you going to die? Of what?

The parables and questions in this guidebook are designed to get you to think. Spiritually, we live in difficult times. We don't have bells ringing every six hours to remind us to stop what we are doing and bow toward Mecca. We need to find other ways to interrupt our lives, to stop several times every day to take a deep breath and meditate or pray. We need to remind ourselves to look for enlightenment today and not to wait for something catastrophic to happen before we stop and think and say, "Oh, now I'm precious and significant and beautiful." We all need bells of mindfulness now.

vi
Prescriptions for Living

I AM A DOCTOR, so when I start telling stories and giving lessons I think of them as prescriptions. In this guide for the perplexed, you will find all the prescriptions you need to deal with the difficulties and afflictions life presents. But you don't have to wait until you are sick to use these prescriptions. You can also think of them as maps to help you find your way.

Will reading this guidebook change you? No. Information does not transform people. You do not heal yourself by reading what your doctor has written on the prescription pad. You do not move because you read a map. Change requires energy, and you must supply the energy. I cannot change you. Only you can change yourself.

Batteries are not included, but directions are. If you have the energy within you, you can follow my directions and find your life's true path. It is unlikely you will lose your way because I will show you shortcuts and warn you of pitfalls and help you maintain your sense of direction. You don't have to get lost to learn your lesson. Others have learned from getting lost, and they can guide, coach and direct you. You can reach your destination on schedule, safe and sound.

> *The first prescription can help you avoid the painful route to wisdom. Many people who experience disaster or a life-threatening illness find the experience awakens them to the beauty of life. Don't wait for disaster to be your teacher. Live more fully now. Ask yourself the questions so many cancer patients ask: What am I here for? What do I want to experience, say and accomplish with the limited time I have left?*
>
> *I mentioned these questions a few pages earlier. This time, do not read them and move on. Spend fifteen minutes answering them. Write your answers down because you'll need them later, and it is surprisingly easy to forget your purpose and what you are here to accomplish.*

vii
Is That How You Live?

WHEN I TELL PATIENTS what I think are their best treatment options, I usually preface my advice with "If I had what you have, this is what I would do."

I have always thought it is fair, when you are confronted with a health problem, to ask your doctor, "Is that what you would want for your wife? Your children? Yourself?" It is also fair to ask the author of a guide for the perplexed, "Is this how you live with your family?" Do you practice what you preach?

Do I follow the prescriptions in this guidebook? Is this

how my family and I live? My wife, Bobbie, and our children appear in many of the stories in this guide, and you'll see from the kinds of things they say that we all try to keep one another grounded and on the path. If I deviate from a loving path, they let me know it. If I'm preaching one thing and living another, they tell me about it. And they are forgiving when they know I am trying and willing to admit my faults.

Bobbie is present at most of the talks I give. Our five children are all grown and out in the world, but they are always invited. Sometimes they attend. They also invite me to speak in areas where they live. So you see, when I get up to speak, I am in front of my family or feel that I am. I could never advise anyone to do anything I am not trying to do. Of course, I sometimes lose my way, but I find that I am able to be helpful to people not in spite of my struggles but because I am struggling with the things I talk about. My pain is my teacher and my family are my directors when I lose my way.

At the hospitals in New Haven where I worked, the nurses would ask in the morning, "Who's here today? Bernie or Dr. Siegel?" If I said, "Dr. Siegel," they would give me a lot of love and help because they knew I was having a tough day. And if I said, "Bernie," they knew they could lighten up because I was okay that day and would be giving hugs.

Sometimes I feel sorry for my wife and children because a quarter century after I turned my desk around and decided to stop being Dr. Siegel, I still am not the person I'd like to be. If I ever become the kind and loving person I want to be, it will be because of them. I am trying to be that person now, but sometimes I'm still Dr. Siegel and I have to keep asking myself, "Well, what would Bernie do now?"

1
Family Matters

i
Jeff's Wisdom

What happy people know that unhappy people don't

OUR SON JEFF lives a half mile from our home. I frequently stop at his house after my morning run or bike ride. We sit on stools in the kitchen and talk about life, both its practical and its philosophical sides. One morning not too long ago, we'd been chatting long enough for me to catch my breath when Jeff asked whether I was writing anything new.

I'm fortunate, I thought, to have a son who is interested in my work. "Yes," I told Jeff, "I'm writing a book about spirituality and how it helps us in difficult times."

"Well," he said, "you should call your book *Holy Shit*."

Walking home from Jeff's house, I thought about Rodney Dangerfield's line, "I don't get no respect." Rodney's complaint is a double negative, and if you think about it a minute and untangle the negatives, you'll see he is actually saying he does not get a lack of respect—so presumably he does get some respect. That seemed fitting to me, because sometimes what appears to be disrespectful ends up being very respectful. That is certainly true in our family, which has always done a lot of teasing. It isn't unusual for the children to remind me not to take myself too seriously, so I was not offended by Jeff's words. They had me thinking, though, and I remembered another time Jeff had offered an enlightening title for one of my books.

A few years earlier, in the same kitchen, he'd told me I should call my next book *Out of My Mind*. My reaction that morning had been to laugh at what I figured was his way of getting in a dig. Why not? He has a father who shaves his head, goes around telling jokes, acts like a child in airports, and writes books about love. But then I realized Jeff's *Out of My Mind* suggestion really was an excellent title. After all, what is there in our lives that doesn't come out of our minds? I've often said that our minds create our feelings. These feelings, depending on their nature, either take their toll on our bodies or help us to remain healthy. How well we deal with difficulties, the quality of our lives, our happiness or misery—it all is determined by what goes on in our minds.

So our son was right, I am out of my mind and that would be a good title. But *Holy Shit*? I thought that one over as I walked home. Yes, Jeff had done it again. Tossing off what sounded at first like an off-the-cuff insult, he'd summarized my message again. Life is holy shit. God may prefer the term "compost" but it amounts to the same thing. We all have our problems but those problems redirect us and teach us to grow. Our difficulties fertilize our lives. The enlightened individual—and the happy family—knows that possibilities grow out of problems. People who know how to be happy say, "Thank you, God, for the fertilizer," while the unhappy cry out, "Oh God, why us?"

As for me, I say, "Thank you God, for our wise son's respectful disrespect."

Tolstoy said that all happy families resemble each other, while each unhappy family is unhappy in its own way. Why is that? All families have problems. Happy families don't escape adversity, they just deal with it better. If they resemble each other, it is because there are only a few ways to be happy in the face of adversity. But there are many unhappy ways to respond to problems—enough that each unhappy family can find its own unique way of being miserable.

Novelists tend to be interested in the unhappy families and the choices they make, just like doctors tend to study patients who get sick and die. But there is more to learn from studying patients who don't die when you expect them to.

As a doctor, I studied survivors—people who got sick but exceeded expectations. Many of those exceptional patients had been given little time to live, yet they were some of the happiest people I'd ever met. They knew, or they discovered through their illness, which became their teacher, that if you want to be happy, you must answer some key questions. What are you here for? And how do you want to spend your limited time? If your answer is that you are here to love, to serve others and not to be served, then you already have everything you need to be happy. If you wake up in the morning, that's enough, you are grateful for life and the opportunity to contribute in your way.

In happy families, loving means accepting. Robert Frost said that home is the place where they always have to take you in. Grandparents know this. A loving family accepts each member as he or she is—even accepts the anger of those who don't feel loved. This can be difficult and it is why I don't recommend having children until you are sixty.

Acceptance won't make the problems go away, and it won't prevent other problems—nothing can do that. As long as your family exists, it will have problems; that's the nature of life and love. Many of your problems will involve your family because you feel safe and can be open and honest with one another.

While you cannot avoid difficulties, you can choose how to

deal with them. You can hope that troublesome family members will change and the problems they are causing will go away. You can try to persuade them of the need for change and end up creating a fine story line for a novelist. Or you can accept them the way they are and choose to love. I have learned you can be devoted to changing someone, or devoted to someone. The latter works better.

ii

Roy and Carolyn's Baby

What a grandfather knows that a doctor didn't

WHEN OUR SON STEPHEN was born, I insisted they let me into the nursery to examine him. The staff resisted at first, and who could blame them? I wasn't asking to hold my son but to examine him. They assured me he was fine, but I was a doctor and I was insistent, so the nurses shrugged and let me in. I checked to be sure Stephen had the correct number of parts and openings, and when I was satisfied he was all there, I gave him back to the nurses and went to keep my wife company.

I had what seemed at the time like a good reason to be worried about Stephen. I was a resident in surgery at the Pittsburgh Children's Hospital. For twelve months I hadn't seen a single normal child. True, there was no reason to think our baby would have any of the problems I'd seen and treated. This was our third child, and the older boys were fine and Bobbie had no problems with this pregnancy or delivery. But the thought of a birth defect in someone I loved troubled me so much as a young father that I couldn't resist examining Stephen as soon as possible.

Later, when I was out in practice, I began to learn a bit about what really matters in life. By the time the twins were born—the fourth and fifth of our five children—I was less of a problem and more of a help to everyone. This was in the days when fathers were not allowed in the delivery room, but they let me listen to the delivery over the intercom. Our only daughter, Carolyn, was born first. Her brother Keith, being a gentleman, came second. This time we did have a reason for concern: Bobbie had been exposed to German measles during the first trimester. But as I said, I'd begun to learn about life and love, so I did not follow the twins to the nursery and insist on examining them.

While I was no longer a compulsive inspector of babies, I still had a lot to learn about being a father. Most of the years our children were growing up I was more concerned with their physical well-being than their spiritual well-being. Yes, I loved them, but I carried a fear inside me: What if they weren't normal? What if they came with—or developed—some terrible physical problem? What would we do then?

It turned out that the twins did have a physical problem—a hearing loss we didn't discover until they were almost five years old and in preschool. They adjusted perfectly well and had healthy childhoods and have followed their older brothers into happy, productive adulthood. Carolyn married a wonderful young man named Roy, and when she became pregnant, she and Roy asked me to be present at the delivery.

As Carolyn's labor progressed, it became evident that the baby was not going to fit into the birth canal. Some of the staff at the hospital who knew me said the problem was his head was as big as his grandfather's. I seem to get blamed for a lot of things. In any event, a cesarean section was indicated. This was at the same hospital where years before I'd listened to Carolyn's birth over the intercom. Although fathers and grandparents were now allowed in the delivery room, only fathers were allowed at a c-section. Roy, however, interceded and insisted that his father-in-law be present.

Roy and I stood by Carolyn's head as the obstetrician made the incision. I watched her lift Patrick's pale, dusky little body up in the air. I saw Patrick take his first breath and heard his first cry and I knew that no matter what he was like I would give him all my love. How many parts or openings he had or didn't have was irrelevant. He had my love and my promise to be there for him no matter what his needs. Thinking about it now, I feel that moment again, and the love and tears well up.

I have not forgotten the deformities I saw every day as a pediatric surgeon at Children's Hospital. I have not forgotten why I examined Steve so thoroughly. I still know that children are born with physical deformities. And I know that the people I love can develop cancer, multiple sclerosis, AIDS—the list is endless. But life has taught me that while much can go wrong, there is little to fear in physical deformities or illnesses. If Bobbie and I had a child today, I would not be worried about how many parts it had. I would simply say, "This is another opportunity for love. If something is missing, it's missing. We'll make the best of it, and who knows what good things we'll learn from this?"

Some young parents already have this attitude and do not worry as I did, but the ability to accept life as it comes is more common among grandparents. It was after Patrick was born and I realized how much better I've become at loving that I decided that people should not become parents until they are sixty—or can behave as if they are. We need to educate parents so they can behave as if they have the wisdom of grandparents.

If the ugly duckling had been lucky enough to have parents as wise as grandparents, he wouldn't have needed to leave home and to look in the lake to see his beautiful reflection. His beauty would have been reflected back in the loving faces of his family.

iii

Groupet Therapy

What your pets know that you don't

I'VE DISCOVERED A FORM OF GROUP THERAPY that is particularly good for people who worry a lot, or have trouble relaxing or accepting life and loving unconditionally. This form of therapy is not yet covered by insurance, but the cost is reasonable and the sessions can be held in your home. I call it groupet therapy.

We all know the benefits of group therapy for a variety of physical and emotional afflictions. Lately pet therapy has been getting a good deal of attention, particularly for senior citizens and the disabled. Groupet therapy is a combination of these approaches. In groupet therapy, you meet once a week with a group of pets. You select the type of pets you want in your group. I personally have entered a feline group because cats are easily available, they fit my schedule, and if we meet in the afternoon they nap a lot so I get to do most of the talking.

People will want to choose different groupets, depending on the issues they need to address. You might choose a canine group when you need to improve your bark, for instance. Reptile therapy works for those who want quiet time for imagery or who like to be surprised by where the group is meeting. If you have an ego problem, you might want to meet with hamsters, who are much smaller than we are and very sociable. If you need help expressing anger, a good hissing session with some snakes can do wonders. Horses are great for those who always get lost on the way home, and Canadian geese can do wonders for people in couples therapy.

My regular group is run by Miracle, a Jewish, black and white, domestic short-haired psychiatrist. Currently the rest of the group includes Dickens, Gabriel, Penny and me.

Dickens is a gray, long-haired Maine Coon Buddhist who meditates a lot and says very little, but when he does speak his wisdom is profound. Gabriel is a red Maine Coon Muslim who faces Mecca more often than the group, even while he is talking.

The group problem is Penny, or Penelope if you want to help her self-esteem. Penny is a Catholic, tortoiseshell, domestic longhair from Our Lady of Perpetual Responsibility. They sent Penny to us to see if we could help her overcome her guilt and phobias. She lost her family as a kitten and grew up in a barn with a phone. Now any bell, even if on television, frightens the wits out of her. She disappears for long periods, even from group sessions, if anyone rings our doorbell. We don't charge for the missed sessions and Miracle always licks her face when she returns.

Last but not least is Bernie, a baldheaded guy from Connecticut who likes to talk. He misses a lot of sessions because of travel, but when he attends groupet sessions he generally is the one who benefits most—probably because he has the most to learn.

What has my groupet taught me in a few short analytical years? They've demonstrated over and over again that we are loved and accepted no matter what our race, creed or color. My pet therapy group knows God loves us all just the way we are and is more concerned with the content than the container. They have taught me to live in the moment. To be less concerned about my appearance. To get outside and enjoy watching birds, squirrels and nature. To see each day as an opportunity to love and nap. To feel no guilt about taking time for myself and not to stare at myself in the mirror.

They have shown me that if you persist in expressing your needs, in a loving way, people will feed and care for you. They keep me company when I'm not well and sit on my paperwork when they know I need a break. And they are always ready at bedtime to keep me warm—without disturbing the covers. I could go on and on about their advantages, some of which are unanticipated.

Just the other day a television producer called to invite me, rather insistently, to come to Boston to tape a show. I didn't want to go to the studio in Boston and invited the producer to send a team to my home instead. She didn't like that idea. In the middle of the negotiations, Gabriel climbed on my desk and stepped on the phone, cutting off the call. I didn't have the producer's phone number, so I waited for her to call back. Ten minutes, fifteen minutes, twenty minutes passed and she didn't call. Too bad, I thought. I did want to do this show— enough that I would have agreed to go to Boston for the taping. Thanks a lot, I told Gabriel, who ignored me and stared off toward Mecca. A few minutes later, the phone rang. The producer was on the line telling me they would come to my house for the taping. I asked if she thought I hung up on her. She said, "Yes, didn't you?" I said, "No." I explained that the cat stepped on the phone, and for that favor Gabriel has a home forever.

I am aware of many other people who have learned from their pets. One woman learned about wholeness from a three-legged cat she adopted. As a kitten, this cat had had a terrible infection and his mother had chewed his leg off to save him. The wound healed and the kitten grew into a cat and seemed perfectly comfortable with three legs. The woman grew used to thinking of her three-legged cat as a complete cat, and she realized what a lesson this was when she found herself sitting in an airport next to a man who had had his arm amputated. Before she adopted her cat, the woman said, she would have lowered her eyes and turned away in embarrassment. But now she thought of her three-legged cat and realized the man next to her was a complete person, and she was comfortable with him and began talking to him, and they had a wonderful conversation.

> *This prescription is actually a referral to groupet therapy. Make an appointment with your pets. If you don't have pets, borrow a friend's, or better yet go to the ASPCA or your local animal shelter and pick up the fellow creatures you need to start a groupet. I guarantee you that whatever your pets are, they know some things about being happy and healthy that you have forgotten or never learned. So spend some time listening to and observing them. Perhaps someday we can create the ASPCH and prevent cruelty to humans. (Definitely no neutering required.)*

iv
Jesus, Buddha, Moses, Gandhi and Lassie

Preparing for the times when perplexity strikes

IT CAN BE HARD to always provide others with what they want. How do you know what your child is looking for when he or she feels unloved? What do you do when you try to help your spouse with the groceries and you put the tomatoes in the refrigerator, only to find a note, "You don't put tomatoes in the refrigerator"? Even with the support of a good therapeutic groupet, it may seem hard at first to know how to respond to a demanding infant, a sullen adolescent, a needy parent, an angry spouse or a howling dog.

We moved into a new house when our children were young. Our son Keith was an angelic child who never caused any trouble, so we gave him a room at the end of the hall. We put the rowdier boys in the rooms closer to us. Years later, I found out that Keith thought we'd put him far away from us because we didn't love him as much. When even your best intentions can go wrong, it is hard to know how to make decisions.

One way to start making decisions is by asking what effect your actions might have on the children. What would a loving mother do in your situation? If you never had a loving mother it may be difficult for you to know how a loving mother would act. In that case, think of role models who could take the loving mother's place. Ask yourself, "What would _____ do now?" Some choices might be Jesus, Buddha, Moses, Abraham, Mother Teresa, Joan of Arc, Mohammed, Confucius, Gandhi.

I sometimes look to those figures for guidance, but I have also found two less renowned role models who work well for me: Don Quixote and Lassie.

Don Quixote reminds me what happens when you decide to view the world through loving eyes. In the show *The Man of La Mancha*, even more than in Cervantes' book, we see the effect love has upon the lover and those around him. Don Quixote's love transforms the downtrodden prostitute Aldonza into the lovely lady Dulcinea. So I use him as a role model when transformation is in order.

But Don Quixote also attacks windmills. Using force, however, does not change the world as the power of love does. Lassie, my other role model, knows how to act tough without actually resorting to force. Lassie helps me remember that it is perfectly acceptable to defend yourself with a growl. A good growl often averts the need to bite anyone. Other times growls are unnecessary, and a leap onto a lap and a lick of the face will do the trick.

If none of your role models provides the answer, then it is time to go within and ask yourself, "What would make me happy?" In other words, let your feelings guide you. This doesn't work well if you focus narrowly on your personal needs. I am not talking about selfishness or self-interest. When I ask, What will make you happy?, I mean, What way of loving others feels right for you? Choose a way of loving that makes you happy, and your efforts will be play rather than work.

Lastly, if nothing has helped you decide, go ask a child. Children know what they need, and more surprisingly, they know what we need. Adults think. Kids respond with their feelings. They don't think about what you will think of their answer, so they just speak the truth—if you can get to them before junior high school age. At that time, they grow up, stop feeling loved, become depressed and start thinking—and what they are thinking about worries me.

It's hard to carry a child around with you, but fortunately, in most cases, you don't have to ask a child for directions if you have a well-chosen role model ready to guide you. This is the next prescription: Take one role model, as often as needed. Set aside a few minutes today to fill this prescription so you will have it handy when you need it. Think now about who your role models have been. What do they offer? Who else do you admire, and exactly what do you admire about them? Have your roster of role models ready and waiting to help you the next time you are perplexed.

v
Relationships

Getting along with yourself and other difficult loved ones

WHEN I SPEAK TO GROUPS I don't give lectures—I talk about my relationships. That could be too big a subject for this book unless I limit it to those who are closest to me. In order of importance, they are my God, my wife, our children, our family, the people we work with and care for and me.

I'll start at the end of the list, with myself, because I am the most difficult person I have to deal with. My goal is to love and to devote myself to everyone on the list, but I often fall far short of that goal. That is why I put God first—because I need God, as Head Professor, to teach me. I'll talk more about getting along with God later when I discuss Abraham and Isaac and some of my teaching assistants, skunk cabbage and earthworms. Meanwhile, how do I get along with myself?

I keep pictures of myself as a child around to help me recall what a precious creation I am and to remind me to be more forgiving of myself. I ask all the people I have relationships with to help keep me on track and to forgive me when I am not. My family does a good job of keeping me on track by reminding me, "You're not in the operating room now." When I received a prestigious award, our son Jonathan helped out by observing, "I guess they've lowered their standards."

Our family tries to offer criticism that is wise, constructive and humorous. Mostly we accept each other's comments and feel safe with each other. Bobbie and I were married in 1954 and by now we know that anger does not mean "I don't love you" or "I want a divorce." It means, "I am wounded and in need of love, and I feel safe telling you about it because you are my family." Sometimes our behavior with each other is no different from the cry of an unattended baby.

Even with the help of God, Bobbie and the family, I have a lot to learn about myself and a long way to go before I can live up to the examples set by Lassie and Don Quixote. I expect to be working on myself up to my last breath. Until then I'll keep trying, and as long as I am trying, I know the family will put up with me.

You need a few very simple things to keep a relationship healthy: a commitment to the relationship, love, devotion and a childlike sense of humor. Then when difficulties arise, as they inevitably will, you have four options. You can eliminate the other person, eliminate yourself or eliminate the relationship. Or you can see the problem as a riddle and solve it by asking how love could heal the relationship.

The first two options can be destructive if carried out literally. You can remove yourself physically without literally eliminating anyone. The third option is divorce, and I recommend it only under specific conditions, which I will explain. If you are willing to try the fourth option divorce may not be necessary.

When would I recommend a divorce? You should leave any relationship in which you are threatened by physical violence. If someone is chasing you around the house with a hatchet, you don't say, "How can love solve this?" You say, "I'm leaving." You also should leave if the marriage is making you physically sick and your spouse is unwilling to change. You deserve to be treated with respect even in difficult times, and you should not stay in a relationship that makes you more vulnerable to disease or injury.

As a general rule, I recommend the fourth choice, which means bringing God into your relationships. If devotion and spirituality are a part of your life, then you will make choices that benefit everyone in the long term. If you view marital problems as riddles, then you will unite to look for solutions. If you see your problems as puzzles, you can always find solutions based on your love, devotion and sense of humor.

The humor part is vital. When your wife, who has spilled hot coffee on you in the past, pours hot herbal tea in your lap, you write a poem thanking her for cutting out the caffeine. When you put all the groceries away and instead of thanking you she complains that you put the tomatoes in the refrigerator, you resist the urge to complain about how unappreciated you are. Instead, you go into your den, sit down and write a poem, just as I did:

Divorce
tomatoes don't belong in the refrigerator
I did it again
my wife may never forgive me
our marriage is on the rocks
I snore, put tomatoes in the fridge
walk and eat too fast
the divorce lawyer doesn't know how to help us reach a
valid settlement
for my cruelty
he suggests we love and try to work it out
and don't put tomatoes in the fridge
I read his settlement to my wife
she laughs
I love her when she laughs

and forget the difficult times
we fire the lawyer
and take the tomatoes out of the fridge

Bobbie did laugh when I read my "Divorce" poem, and I do love her when she laughs. Then, together, we did take the tomatoes out of the fridge.

After family, the next people on my list are the people we work with and care for. The key here is understanding that these relationships require the same sort of loving care that keeps family relationships healthy. Treat people with respect, listen to them and above all remember that they have problems, too. They, too, may need your help when they are hurting.

Bobbie remembers the need to give love, and it makes a world of difference to me. Before leaving for the airport on a recent trip, I went shopping and ran some errands to be a helpful husband. When I came home I balanced the shopping bag on a waste basket while I cleaned the four kitty litter containers. The grocery bag fell, spilling various sticky liquids on the floor and making such a mess that even the cats fled. I bellowed "Poor me!" and moaned about my difficult life and difficult wife. When I opened my luggage that evening in my hotel room, there was the note Bobbie always manages to sneak in. "Thank you very much for all the effort. Love you very much," and then there were kisses (XXX) from Bobbie and the cats, who also appreciated my efforts with the kitty litter. The note was a simple touch, but it healed me because it really did let me know that even when I'm making a mess, Bobbie notices my effort and appreciates it.

Whenever our daughter, Carolyn, types for me on the computer, she always signs off with, "I love you Mom and Dad."

She is like her mom, who always leaves love notes. Every time I see the message from Carolyn or find one of Bobbie's notes in my suitcase, I feel like I've been handed a dozen roses.

I offer this as a short, simple and sweet prescription. Say it now! Not when you learn you have little time left to live. Don't say it with a big bouquet and a long, eloquent, dramatic eulogy at the funeral. Give a reminder of your love to someone in your family today. A note, flowers, card, pin or hug, or just say it out loud. Your spouse, a child, a parent—everyone in the family needs reminders. Say "I love you" today, starting with the one who is hardest to say it to and who needs a bouquet the most. Your Aldonza will become a Dulcinea. I guarantee it. This prescription always works and has no adverse side effects.

vi
I'm Sorry I Love You
The fine points of apologizing

ONE MORNING BEFORE SCHOOL our five children were eating breakfast and were a lot noisier and more aggressive than usual. As the name-calling and teasing got more intense, I called everyone to order and suggested they apologize for hurting one another's feelings. I reminded them that when I was upset with any of them and expressed my feelings, I never left the house without saying, "I'm sorry. I love you."

"You're sorry you love us?" one of the children repeated, perplexed.

"No," I said. "I mean, 'I'm sorry.' Period. 'I love you.' Period."

When I'd clarified the punctuation, the children nodded with relief and went back to their sibling squabbling.

Sincerely offered and properly punctuated, an apology can heal wounds and repair relationships. I have seen long-standing family conflicts resolved when one family member is willing to say, "I am sorry. I love you." The apologies that heal relationships are heartfelt, are supported by action and sometimes need to be repeated a number of times.

When people offend me by their behavior, or disappoint me by doing poor work, I let them know it. This can be my doctor, my plumber or the hotel staff when I travel. If the response is a simple, unadorned apology, I accept it and we start our relationship anew. I do not accept apologies that are qualified by a list of reasons that the offense really wasn't the apologizer's fault. That does not heal my wounds. Explanations don't help. The apologizer's sorrow and sincerity are what heals.

We travel a lot and have had several disastrous hotel stays. In one hotel the concierge asked what she could do to make up for the bad service we'd received. I said, "Take us home with you." She said, "I can't because we are short-staffed and I have to work another shift, but I will see that you are taken care of." We laughed. I adopted her into our family and felt healed. Later that evening I told the woman who delivered our meal that I was related to the concierge. She said, "My daughter is married to her son. So we are all family."

We all have our troubles and when we are hungry or hurting we may behave in ways that offend others. Offering so-called legitimate explanations doesn't do as much good as simply saying, "I'm sorry I offended you."

Kindness is a spiritual choice. Don't wait until you are almost dead to heal your relationships. Make no excuses. Place no blame. Just apologize, with sincerity and with correct punctuation, and you and the person you offended can move on or not. You have created a setting of *at-one-ment*. It is up to the other person now to find peace or not.

vii
Forgiving

Do I forgive, or forget, and does it matter?

OFTEN WHEN SOMEONE APOLOGIZES the other person will accept the apology by saying, "Oh, forget it."

But do forgetting and forgiving have the same result?

This is an important question because forgiveness is at the heart of a healthy and happy life. Forgiveness protects relationships. It also protects the person who does the forgiving. Remember the story that psychiatrist and author Robert Coles tells about Ruby, the little girl who integrated a Southern elementary school. Every day the federal marshals had to escort Ruby through a mob of adults who spat at her and called her hateful names. Remarkably, the five-year-old girl did not seem to be emotionally damaged by the ordeal, a fact that puzzled Coles until he discovered that Ruby prayed every day asking God to forgive her persecutors.

But what is forgiveness? Is it the same as forgetting?

Forgetting has to do with self-interest or personal gain. We want to be free of disturbing memories, so we try to put troubling events behind us. Forgetting is a misguided method *for getting* peace of mind. It is, when well done, like amnesia. When you forget your past you can interact, in the present, with the people or things from your past that created a problem.

The problem is, what you forget doesn't necessarily go

away. Burying something in your backyard only hides it from view. The things you forget may be buried beneath the ground of consciousness, but they live on beneath the surface and manifest themselves in your feelings and activities. They show up in your dreams and your drawings and continue to be part of your life, whether you are aware of them or not. You are better off remembering troubling events, feeling the effects of the memory, and resolving the problem in a way that leads to true healing. This can only happen when you forgive.

Forgiveness is a method *for giving* love. It is a way of saying, "I am going to let go of the wrong you did; I am not going to be bitter and I am going to go on loving you anyway." When we forgive we achieve the peace of the gods and become like gods. God has no unforgivable sins, only people do. Remember the hymn that ends, "He'll always say, 'I forgive.'" It doesn't say, "He'll always say, 'I forget.'" Forgiveness allows us to go on loving and to begin healing. It is in for-giving that we receive.

God has three plaques over Her desk. I'll tell you about the second and third ones later. The first plaque says, "Everything you forget I remember, and everything you remember I forget." Why? Because God knows that forgetting means that injuries and wounds will not heal. They will fester beneath the surface and lead to ill health—mental, physical and spiritual. Ruby could not have protected herself by forgetting how the howling mob was treating her—forgiveness was the only thing that could protect her. Every time we forgive, we begin a new life, free of the past and open to love. Remember, forgiveness is not only about your relationship with others but also about your relationship with yourself.

You are here to serve, not to be served. All the holy prophets agree, we are here for giving, not for getting. So try forgiving someone today. Spend some time remembering something

you've tried to forget, some wrong that has been done to you.
Remember, think, feel, understand and then forgive. If the act
of forgiving is hard, forgive yourself first. This takes practice. I
am going to prescribe forgiveness several more times, and I'll
suggest some ways you can get better at forgiving. But for now,
it is enough to stop forgetting and start forgiving.

viii
Responsibility

The sixty percent solution

IT'S MY FAULT. The cat litter hasn't been changed. It's February
and the storm windows aren't up. The lights were left on last
night. The television, too. Tonight we have to give a talk and
we haven't had time to open the mail. Yesterday you forgot
your dentist's appointment and missed *Seinfeld*. And it's all my
fault.

Most of what goes wrong around our house is my fault. I
insist on that, because when I lay claim to our problems and
apologize for them my wife agrees that I am the problem and
she becomes even more forgiving than usual. So it's my fault
the lights were on all night, and I'm sorry.

This, I've discovered, is the formula for a successful relationship: Assume the majority of the responsibility. If you
accept sixty percent of the responsibility and your mate does,
too, you will have a wonderful relationship.

Once you accept responsibility, you can stop wasting time
debating who is at fault and start growing. You can become
more aware of what you are doing and stop blaming others for

your reactions to their actions. We need to remind ourselves what we tell our children: Nobody "makes" you do anything—you are responsible for your actions. No matter what your brother/sister/husband/wife does, you have a choice how you respond. So choose, take responsibility, and have a healthy relationship.

I discovered the sixty percent solution some years ago, but like all prescriptions it occasionally needs adjusting. Not long ago my wife and I were sitting side-by-side on the sofa discussing something and I said, "You're impossible." Bobbie responded, "No dear, I'm next to impossible." She's right, and I love her, so I now accept seventy-five percent of the responsibility, and I'm working my way up. After all, Joseph Campbell and my wife agree: Marriage is an ordeal and a struggle because you are creating a relationship, a new entity, devoid of self-interest.

ix
No, No, No, No, No

Choosing how you will contribute love

WILL YOU TAKE ME to dinner tonight? Can you come to my basketball game? Read me a bedtime story? Bring in the groceries? Can we count on you to serve on the finance committee?

All good questions, and the correct answers for you may be no, no, no, no and no.

How do you feel when you see those words? Is it hard for you to say no—especially when the request comes from someone you love? Are you hurt when someone says no to you? One of the great lessons we learn from our mortality is the importance of saying no.

Saying no to requests from the ones you love is not selfish—not when you say no in order to choose a different way of contributing your love to the world. Saying no defines you and your boundaries. It does not mean you have no empathy or compassion for others. It means you do have concern—some for them and some for yourself.

It is no accident that God let Adam and Eve eat from the tree of knowledge and not the tree of life. Yes, he did *let* them eat the forbidden fruit. Think a minute: God has an orchard and can't figure out how to keep two people out? You can't hide from God, so let's understand that this was thought out by God. But God let us eat the fruit that gave us not immortality, but knowledge of our nudity and our mortality.

Adam and Eve quickly figured out that a leaf or a designer garment can eliminate the nudity problem, but nothing makes our mortality problem go away. So why did God let us discover this problem? The Creator must have known that if we were aware of our mortality, we would think about our lives, value our lifetimes and become much wiser.

I have worked with a lot of people who have life-threatening illnesses, and when they faced death, they all discovered the same thing: Time isn't money, it's everything. Spend it on who and what you love.

Read the story of Adam and Eve eating from the tree of knowledge, and remember that you, too, are going to die. Decide how much of your limited time you want to spend being unhappy. If something is bothering you and you know you are mortal, you'll find ways to resolve the problem.

With your death in mind, think about the things people have asked you to do in the last twenty-four hours. Ask yourself what will happen if you try to meet every one of those requests. Is this the way you want to contribute your love? If you decide you are not saying no often enough, find a place to say no once before the end of the day. When you do say no to your loved ones, make it clear that a no to one of their requests is sometimes a yes to love and life.

x
Burn Up or Burn Out

Creativity versus destruction

WHAT IS THE DIFFERENCE between a person who is burning out and one who is burning up? How does a workaholic affect the lives of those around him, compared with a creative person going joyfully about his work?

If you are giving your all to life and you feel exhausted, it may be hard to tell whether you are working hard or you have become a workaholic. An easy, painless test will reveal whether you are burning up or out: Take a nap. If you are burning up, you will be restored. Rest will recharge your battery and allow you to resume your activity, and your work will be a beacon for others to follow. If you are burning out, you do not light the way for others, and no matter how much physical rest you get you still feel fatigued.

The workaholic loses interest in life-enhancing activity (and probably won't want to take a nap, even as an experiment). Workaholics are addicted to the act of working and have lost sight of the reasons for working. They no longer care what effect their work has on other people. The work is destructive because it comes before everything else and demands that everything and everyone must be sacrificed. Ultimately, workaholics destroy their own lives and the lives of others. They are working for the wrong lord—a destructive one.

When you are doing work that burns you out, you are busy and you have only *outsight*, the concern about what others see in you. But when you are burning up, you are creating and you have insight into yourself and your life. With inner sight, you will make fewer mistakes and have fewer accidents.

If you are creative, your work is play no matter how hard you are working. Creators lose track of time because they love what they are doing—and if you lose track of time you can't age. Your body chemistry changes during periods of creativity. You truly don't age because of your physiology. You are in a trance state and unaware of your body. If I have a backache or a running injury, it disappears while I am working at something I love. When I give lectures, perform surgery or do something with my family, any pain I had goes away. When the act of love is over, the pain returns. That's the wonderful part of burning up: You can't be sick when you are burning up, because your physiology is altered while you are wrapped up in creative work. You are having a near-life experience.

A woman once wrote me to say she'd been told she was dying so she made out a will, gave away treasures, bought a dog, took vitamins, laughed more, put in a backyard wildlife habitat. Her letter ended with "I didn't die and now I'm so busy I'm killing myself." When you do what you love it is therapeutic. I told her to take a nap.

Manifest your creativity. Do what you love and you'll be amazed at how much you get done. And no matter how hard you work, you will need only every seventh day off. You may want to interrupt your six workdays for battery-charging naps or rests so you can stop and see that what you are doing is good.

And now a prescription to go along with saying no: Take a nap. Napping is not only good medicine, it is an important diagnostic tool.

xi
Encouragement

The helium of life

WHAT IS THE THING that can make your life feel like a balloon ride? What brings you the sensation of floating free, silently carried by the wind? What lifts your spirits and allows you to overcome difficulties? The answer is very simple: encouragement.

That's right, encouragement. Not success. Knowing that our efforts are appreciated is more important than being successful. Encouragement removes the burdens we carry and allows us to go on with confidence. Hemingway is supposed to have said that confidence is the memory of past success, and I agree that success can beget success. But think about very young children: They don't have any past successes. If we need success to be successful, then how did any of us ever learn to walk? What made you get up again, each time you fell? You got up and tried again because your parents held out their hands and encouraged you to try. "You can make it," they said. Walk. Use a spoon. Ride a bike. Think of the things you learned because your parents encouraged you. Watch a child learn to crawl, walk and play ball again after surgery for a brain tumor, and you'll see how important encouragement is.

The key element in encouragement is to stop being judgmental. The important thing isn't the grade your son got; it's the effort he put out. It isn't whether your daughter hit a home run; it's that she went up to the plate and took a swing. The effort is what matters, because as long as we are trying we are fulfilling our mission. "Examine me, O Lord, and try me," the Psalmist wrote.

In the book *Tuesdays with Morrie*, the author Mitch Albom writes about his former college professor, who was dying of amyotrophic lateral sclerosis. The ailing professor went to a basketball game where the students started yelling, "We're number one, we're number one." He climbed down out of the stands, walked out on the court and said to the student body, "What's wrong with being number two?"

We are not always going to be number one, but we are almost always better than we think we are. Most of us just don't give ourselves enough credit—we are kinder, smarter, even better looking than we think. Bobbie and I have videos we made from our forty-year-old home movies, and it is a shock now to look at them. I look at those videos and I can't get over how beautiful my wife is, and I can't figure out why she married me. But then I look at myself and I'm amazed to see that I didn't look that bad either—not as good as Bobbie, but not bad. I say, "Hey, that's a pretty good-looking kid." Would I like to be that kid? Yes. But did I like the way I looked then? No. As a twenty-year-old, I looked in the mirror and all I saw were my faults.

Our children are better than they think, too. What kind of mirror do we hold up to them? Do we point out all their faults and problems, or do we point out their beauty and successes? What do you say to your kids when they walk out the door? Stand up straight? Fix your pants? Did you forget your lunch or your books? Do you ever say, "You're a beautiful person. God and I are proud of you."

A friend tells me he tries to encourage his children, but his fourteen-year-old daughter doesn't believe him when he tells her how wonderful she is. Two-year-olds don't doubt you when you hold out your hands and tell them they can walk, but it can be trickier encouraging older children or spouses or adult friends. Giving encouragement, like other forms of loving, sometimes requires creativity.

Most of us grow up being told not to lie, and become very good at it so people won't know we are doing it. We learn to look one another in the eye and swear we never did or said such a thing. So our teenagers don't believe the encouraging things we say to them because they no longer trust us.

But we do believe what people say when we overhear something that wasn't meant for our ears. I once overheard my father saying nice things about me. If he'd told me to my face that I was going to be a success in life, I probably would have said, "Sure, Dad, right, thanks," and then would have promptly forgotten his remarks. From the other room, I heard him say to my aunts and uncles, "That kid'll be a success at anything he does." I've remembered those words all my life and have always felt uplifted by his faith in me.

Suppose your daughter comes to you and says, "I'm going out tonight. How do I look?" Of course you answer, "Beautiful." Maybe you do think she looks terrific and when she's out the door, you say to her mother, "That kid is a knockout. She could be a model. Aren't we fortunate to have such a beautiful kid?" Or maybe when she's out the door you throw up your hands and say, "What's with the ring through her eyebrow and exactly what color is her hair now?"

If your daughter happens to have forgotten something and is standing at the door, the words she overhears—for better or worse—will mean a lot more to her than the words you spoke to her.

Here is a prescription for encouraging the people you love: Say good things about them to their faces and behind their backs. And don't worry about exaggerating. An overdose of love has no recorded adverse side effects. I am speaking for a higher authority when I tell you that. If you need proof, see I Corinthians 13 in your Bible.

xii
Acceptance

Our Grandson, the Pope

ENCOURAGING PEOPLE DOESN'T DO MUCH GOOD if you then turn around and tell them their decisions and efforts are no good. The whole point of encouragement is to help your loved ones make their own decisions. Some of those decisions will differ from the ones you might have made. They may choose work that isn't what you wish they had chosen, but it's their life.

Several of our children have married outside my faith. Would I prefer they marry within their religion? Yes, because I know that marrying outside the family faith will very likely bring them more problems—but not from me. My job is to accept them and love them, not to criticize them and make their lives more difficult. It has been easier for our third, fourth and fifth children because our first two taught me to let them live their lives and not my desires.

I was brought up in the Jewish faith and I enjoy its traditions, rituals and laws. I like being able to talk to God with no intermediaries, to study Jewish mysticism and to read the interpretations of the laws by the great rabbis of the past. This makes it dynamic for me and open to review, like a Supreme Court case. The wisdom of the past helps me to live today.

I know that our children must find their own way. I didn't have that hard a time accepting their decisions about faith because I have incorporated the wisdom of many religions into my own life. Today I would describe myself as a Confucian, Shamanic, Christian, Buddhist, Muslim, Hindu, Quaker, Taoist Jew. If I left anyone's religion out, there is no need to be offended. Please send me a note and I'll study your faith, too.

My interest in other people's religions hasn't kept me out of trouble with some of the faithful. Some fundamentalists have called me satanic and occultic because I teach imagery and meditation. They are concerned that the devil may appear when one's eyes are closed. This confuses me because the Bible tells us it is God who speaks to us in dreams and visions. But I'm not looking for arguments, so I just tell people to keep their eyes open for the devil when they are napping or doing imagery. I agree it is a good idea to be on the lookout at all times for evil, but we also need to get some rest or we will lose our way.

Our grandson Patrick has been circumcised and baptized. These are acts performed because of his parents' faith, so that he can be part of a group that professes certain beliefs. You'd think this would mean he'll find acceptance everywhere, but instead he'll probably make people of both traditions unhappy. There are members of Patrick's own family who are bothered by his parents' decision to have him baptized and circumcised. I guess I am more Buddhist in this respect, because love and kindness are the basis of my religious beliefs. The rituals and outward signs are not as important as one's actions and deeds. Religion should be a path to God, not something to fight about. As long as Patrick's parents are raising him with love and kindness, I am not going to worry about how they work out the details.

I wonder, though, how the family will feel if Patrick becomes pope when he grows up. I hope his circumcision won't rule him out. Personally, I would be very proud and wish him well. He would have a chance to help the world find peace and love, and I am sure I'd be lecturing with pride about my grandson the pope. It's not so unlikely, you know. If you look back in the history of the Catholic Church you will find one of our boys played a very prominent role.

xiii

Accepting Help

Keep your eye on the road

ANOTHER FORM OF ACCEPTANCE is accepting help—which sometimes is a good idea even when you don't need it. I let Bobbie help me constantly when we are in the car and I am driving. Whether I need it or not, she always reminds me to watch the road ahead and not the scenery.

It is easy to live with our eyes focused on the scenery of the past and not on what lies ahead. Where you are and where you have been is important, but it is more important to be aware of where you are going, just as Bobbie reminds me. The future doesn't come to us by chance—we prepare our futures, both consciously and unconsciously. You can sometimes see in people's dreams and drawings the future they are creating for themselves.

What kind of future are you preparing for yourself? Where are you going? Is it where you want to be? You have an internal map. Take it out, unfold it, and see if you are going where you are supposed to be going. Are you open to the signs and traffic directions placed before you?

If you have trouble following your own internal directions, try this method that Bobbie came up with to help me. On long trips when she wants to take a nap, she puts a tape in the car's tape player. While she sleeps, the tape reminds me: "Stay awake. Keep your eyes on the road. Don't look at the map while you're driving. Pull over and stop if you need to read the directions. Slow down. Be careful. Watch the car next to you. Do you need to stop for coffee? Please adjust the heater or air conditioner. Do you need to stop for gas? I need to use the bathroom. Are you awake? Please stop at the next rest area."

Sometimes I pop her tape out when she is sleeping and put on gospel music because it gives me a better sense of direction.

Bobbie hasn't made a tape for my lectures yet because my mistakes are unpredictable. She'll interrupt to correct my English or tell me that something I described as taking sixteen hours really took only fourteen. After one of her corrections I usually point out to everyone what our marriage is like and the audience roars. The truth is, I had to learn that Bobbie was making me a better person with her directives and I now honor them. It has taken her more than forty years, but I now sing on key, sometimes. We all need directors.

Find what gives you direction and pay attention to the road ahead. If you discover you don't like the way things are going, remember that you chose the road you are traveling, and you can always choose another. I find the best roads are marked with whimsy and creativity—the kind of signposts that attract a child's attention—but that's the next part of the story. As Yogi Berra said, "When you come to a fork in the road, take it."

2

Children, Creation and the Voice of God

i

Something from Nothing

The one thing that solves all your problems

WHEN ROB MARRIED NANCY, we were unable to attend the wedding, but we sent a special gift to their California home: We sent them nothing.

Why would we send two lovely people a card saying, "Congratulations. Here's nothing"?

Rob is our daughter-in-law Judy's brother, and his new wife, Nancy, is a charming and talented actress. We are fond of Rob and Nancy, and happy to have them in our extended family. We chose their gift carefully, following our guideline for helping the family celebrate birthdays, anniversaries or weddings. We try to give gifts that show our love and meet people's needs. We thought Rob and Nancy needed nothing, so that is what we gave them—with a card enclosed to explain the value of nothing.

Why is nothing so valuable? Because people who have everything desire nothing. Nothing makes everyone happy. Nothing solves all your problems, and nothing meets everyone's needs.

You can learn a lot about life when someone gives you nothing to think about. Think about the earth you are standing on and all that walks and crawls and grows upon it. Think about the origin of life. Where did the planet and the life on it come from? What preceded us and created us? The only answer scientists give us is "nothing."

Whether you are a philosopher who deals with consciousness or an astronomer who studies dark holes, most people end up having to account for something arising out of nothing. We know that an undifferentiated source of intelligence can give rise, out of nothing, to consciousness, energy, matter and love. We know it can, because it did. So obviously nothing is not the whole story. There is something to nothing which makes it such a valuable gift. Nothing has the potential to become something. That is why many people such as the American Indian place great importance on an all-white animal. It is the blank canvas that reminds us that wherever we have nothing we have the opportunity to create something.

I think it is unlikely we will ever be able to explain fully the first miracle in which everything living arose from nothing. In our age, many scientists reject that which can't be fully explained. But the inexplicable happens all the time. It makes more sense to simply accept things we observe but cannot understand. It is really more scientific to keep an open mind. Until we can understand and explain the things we now label miracles, let us accept them and try to create more of them.

I know from experience and from observing and listening to other people's stories that we can do miraculous things sometimes. We can bring about healing and new life because the loving intelligence that created us out of nothing is still there for all of us to see and use. Ask and you will receive. Believe and it shall be given. Energy and matter are interchangeable, the physicists tell us, and desire and intention alter them.

Did Rob and Nancy appreciate the gift we gave them? A month later we received a note thanking us for a set of silverware. We wrote back saying they had made a mistake and were thanking us for something someone else had sent them. We again pointed out how something can cause embarrassing errors and problems, while nothing keeps everyone out of trouble.

But in case they were not yet ready to appreciate *having* nothing, this time we sent a large, colorful hammock so the two of them could lie down, rest and *do* nothing.

ii

What Could Be Better than Amnesia?

The one thing that brings peace of mind

SEVERAL YEARS AGO I fell off the roof and hit my head on the pavement. When I regained consciousness a beautiful woman was kneeling over me saying, "Honey, are you all right?" I asked her, "Why are you calling me honey?" and she said, "I'm your wife." Then she introduced me to five wonderful children and told me they were ours. After a while she helped me into the house, which was a fascinating place filled with pets and plants and interesting paintings. The reason everything appeared so wonderful was that I had amnesia. I couldn't remember anything that any one of these dear people had ever done to annoy me. Then after a year of bliss my memory returned and I needed counseling.

Since my fall from the roof I've often thought how convenient it would be to awaken with amnesia each day. We wouldn't have to worry about forgiving anyone for anything because we would have no idea what anyone had done.

But there are certain drawbacks to having amnesia. For instance, you don't remember the loving things people have done or the joy you've experienced with the people you love. Fortunately, amnesia is not the only way to achieve peace of mind. The counselor I began seeing when my memory returned told me there is something else that has all the benefits of amnesia and none of its limitations. See if you know what it is.

It is kind and never envious. It is never boastful, or conceited, or rude; never selfish; not quick to take offense. It keeps no score of wrongs and does not gloat over other people's sins, but delights in the truth. There is nothing it cannot face. There is no limit to its faith, its hope and its endurance. It will never come to an end. It is greater than faith and hope. If you do not have it you are nothing no matter what else you may know, or do or have.

You may recognize this wonderful thing and the description I am paraphrasing from I Corinthians 13. I want to thank my counselor for pointing it out and St. Paul, the author of the letter to the Corinthians, for his description of the one thing that is better than amnesia for bringing peace and joy into your life. St. Paul is right. If you have love, you have everything. Without love, you have nothing.

I know two ways to achieve peace of mind. But I am not going to tell you to give yourself a knock on the head to induce amnesia. The side effects of that prescription are too dangerous. Instead, read I Corinthians 13 for a detailed description of the only thing that can bring peace of mind without side effects. You may have read this description of love before. Perhaps you heard it at a wedding. Unless you have read it in the past week, get a Bible and read it again today and don't wait for a knock on the head to wake you up.

iii

Grow Down

The wisdom of children

LOVE. ACCEPT THE MIRACULOUS. Be open to possibilities. Take part in the ongoing act of creation.

We've heard all this before. We know we should love one another and enjoy creation. But how? That's the hard part. St. Paul was feuding with some of the other apostles when he wrote the famous love passage in Corinthians, and the people he was writing to were arguing among themselves. It is one thing to know that love is the key to a life of peace and joy, but it is another thing to be loving.

If you want to become more loving, I can tell you where to find good teachers. Animals can teach us a lot about living in the moment and appreciating the day. About being in the right relationship with God and your fellow creatures. About not being affected by money and not moaning and whining about problems.

If you want human teachers, I can tell you where to find them, too. At lectures and seminars I tell people they'd be happier if they grew down rather than up. My adult audiences usually agree when I go on to explain that many grown-ups aren't very good company. We listened when people told us, "Grow up. Get serious." We have a limited view of the world. There is a sadness about us. We grew up, got serious and became depressed adults.

Prophets, mythmakers and storytellers all advise us to be more childlike. Who inherits the kingdom of heaven? Who sees the truth about the emperor's new clothes? Who lives a timeless life? As a parent and physician, I have learned that when you lose the ability to be childlike you put your life and your health in danger. Children, sick or well, can teach us about honesty and feelings. They can show us how to be loving in the face of adversity and even death. I have seen many children beat cancer—some by getting well and others by living fully despite the cancer that ended their young lives early. Many children with cancer have written letters and some have written books telling what they learned from being sick, and those letters and books are some of the wisest writings I've ever read.

I saw the wisdom of children in my own family many years ago when it appeared that our son Keith, at the age of seven, had cancer. He had complained about his leg hurting and finally, at his urging, we took an X-ray that showed a defect in the bone. I immediately assumed cancer. As a physician, I knew that the only treatment available was an amputation, and that even with this treatment our beautiful child would probably be dead in a year. He was scheduled for surgery to biopsy the tumor, but in the week before his biopsy I viewed him as dead-within-a-year.

I was already living in a tragic future, mourning a death that hadn't yet occurred. I couldn't play with the children or have any fun or make love because I thought I knew what was going to happen. I wanted to tell all the children in the house, "Be quiet. Go to your rooms. Your brother is going to be dead in a year."

The children knew something was wrong with their brother, and they knew it might be serious. But they didn't know the statistics so they did not live in a tragic future. They went about playing, having fun, living each day as it came and not worrying about events that might or might not happen. For that week, I was separated from the family by my grief. Then the biopsy results came back and the tumor was a rare but totally benign growth. So our beautiful son was not dead-within-a-year and I was able to rejoin the family. Keith told me I had handled things poorly. I agreed because I needed him as my teacher. The experience helped me understand what the parents of my patients go through, and it also taught me the folly of living in the future.

You may have heard about living today, tomorrow or "tonow." Tonow, children tell us, is a gift, which is why we call it "the present." Children understand that tonow is the place to live. The present is really the only moment we have. Sure, bad things can happen in the tonow. But when bad things happen to children, they show us the way again, because they know how to be in touch with their feelings and needs.

In the last few decades psychologists have studied survival behavior: Why does one person survive when another in the same circumstance perishes? In war or in accidents or in illness, are there attitudes and behaviors that increase our chances of surviving? I became interested in this question in my work with cancer patients, and over the years I've collected lists of survival traits. When I give lectures I sometimes read one of my lists and ask people to guess what spiritual or self-help group teaches this particular set of maxims:

Tell the truth.

Do your best no matter how trivial the task.

Choose the difficult right over the easy wrong.

Look out for the group before you look out for yourself.

Don't whine or make excuses.

Judge others by their actions and not by their race or other characteristics.

Audiences make all kinds of interesting guesses about which self-help group produced such a wonderful list, but I've only had one person come up with the right answer. "The United States Marines," a man called out one night. He wasn't guessing; he was an ex-Marine, and he remembered what his instructors had taught him about survival behavior.

Children don't have drill sergeants to teach them survival skills, but they know intuitively how to deal with illness and other threatening situations. They know it is good to ask—and even to bellow—for help and love. Adult patients and their families often need to be told that it is healthy and life-enhancing to express emotions. Feelings that are not expressed get stored inside where they become destructive. When you tell adults this, they are not surprised. Yes, they say, I know it is unhealthy to repress my feelings. But they do it anyway. Children, on the other hand, go ahead and express their feelings freely. Infants are the real experts. Toddlers are very good and older children are fair. But by the time we become adults we need to be reminded that feelings should be expressed, and that noise and love can coexist.

Here is another list of survival traits. This list was compiled from the works of many different authors, all of whom had a common experience. See if you can guess what they have in common.

Live life to the fullest; no one knows what will happen tomorrow.

Accept what comes; use it to master the art of living.

Worrying won't help.

Live one day at a time.

Share hope with people.

Remember there's a light at the end of the tunnel.

No one knows the power of the individual.

Keep trying.

It's all right to show emotions.

Don't stop dreaming.

God is always there to help.

Don't wait for tragedy, say it today: "I love you and I'm glad you are alive."

What do the authors of those twelve pieces of wisdom have in common? For one thing, the authors are all children. No doubt you are familiar with some of these maxims. You can find similar messages in popular songs or storybooks. I know I had heard most of their suggestions twenty years ago when I thought our son had cancer, but I certainly didn't *act* as if I knew the value of living one day at a time.

Children who contributed these items are not simply repeating platitudes from songs or storybooks. They know what they are talking about, because each author has or had a life-threatening cancer. I've been fortunate enough to meet some of these children, and I consider them my teachers because they live the message as faithfully as Marines live theirs.

> *Most of us are not in life-threatening situations, but we need a list of survival characteristics for day-to-day life, too. Look at the Marine Corps list and the list written by children with cancer. Both are wise, but there are differences.*
>
> *Read over both lists and commit to memory the items that apply to your life. Add any that you feel are missing. Now you have a short list of behaviors that can help you successfully through the coming week. Before you put the list away, do a self-inventory: Do you act as if you believe in the traits and behaviors on your list? Which of your survival traits are undercut by a negative or destructive list you have been playing in your head? If you need help, join a survivors' group or enlist in the Marines.*

iv

A Work of Art

Where to find love, beauty and honesty

HOLD AN INFANT UP in front of an auditorium full of people, and I guarantee that you will get two responses. One is a group sigh and the other is applause. Why do people react this way to an infant? Because they are beholding a work of art and unlimited potential. When you think about an entire infant arising from one cell, you realize you are looking at an awesome act of creation, a beautiful blossom from a tiny seed.

I once heard Jean Houston say that a child is not a plastic toy violin but a Stradivarius. Why do we lose this sense of awe about ourselves as we grow? We were all beautiful babies once—not necessarily cute or flawless, but beautiful. Those people in the auditorium are not sighing and clapping at the baby's physical appearance, but at its divine nature. A Stradivarius may be out of tune occasionally, but it is still a Stradivarius and it can be tuned. We recognize the innate beauty instinctively with infants, but for some reason we lose the sense of awe about ourselves and other former babies.

If I hold an adult up in front of a high school auditorium, how do you think the students respond? When I speak at schools, I often hold up a baby first and then a student, and people sigh and then laugh. But older students and adults are awesome acts of creation, too. We should view ourselves as artists view their work. They understand that creation is about process and progress. You can paint over a canvas. You can put the clay back on the potter's wheel. And you can rework yourself with the same sense of continued creativity, if you remember that you began as an infant and keep a sense of the infant alive within you.

We travel a great deal, and I love interacting with children at the airport. They look out at the world with a clarity and a directness we adults have lost. Only a child would look at my shaved head and walk up to me and ask, "May I rub your head?" I always agree but I ask for a favor in return. I ask if I can play with one of their toys or if they will sing a song for me. They usually agree. Can you imagine having that negotiation with a grown-up?

Children are wonderful company because they are honest and curious and busy exploring the world. Once when a child walked by me in an airport and dropped a package of gum, I picked it up and held on to it. When the child realized he had lost his gum and saw that I had it (I was acting as if I didn't know whose gum it was), he walked over and asked for his gum. I returned it to him but told him how sad I was to not have any gum. He walked away and then stopped, turned and handed me some sticks of gum. I reached into my bag and gave him one of the pins I always carry with me that says, "You Make a Difference." Then his parents and I had a wonderful talk.

One time I saw a little fellow eating a pretzel that was almost as big as he was. I asked him for a piece. He shook his head no, but then, instead of hiding it from me and finishing it, he walked over to his father, who was looking out the window at the planes coming in. The little guy jerked on his father's pants leg to get his attention.

"What is it?" Dad said, looking down, seemingly annoyed by the interruption.

"Do you have any extra money to buy him a pretzel?" He pointed at me to let his dad know I needed a pretzel, too. That is love. That is beauty. That moment still touches me and makes living worthwhile. In an idle moment in an airport, I had the chance for a moment to play with a Stradivarius, and it made the music of life.

v

True Enlightenment

Thinking about your last fifteen minutes

THE STUDENTS OF AN ENLIGHTENED MONK walked up to him as he was working in his garden and asked, "If you knew you had only fifteen minutes left to live, what would you do, master?" The monk smiled, said "This," and went back to his gardening.

The students were, of course, very impressed with the monk. They understood that his answer meant he was spending every moment of his life doing exactly what was right for him to do.

I am not so impressed with the monk because I am not sure of his answer and whether it shows enlightenment. I think it may show that he was trying to impress his students. I hope I am wrong about him.

The morning after I read about the enlightened monk I stopped by Jeff's house after my run and asked what he would do if he suddenly found out he had fifteen minutes to live. He said, "I'd go get a quart of chocolate ice cream and eat it."

Now that is true enlightenment. Jeff may be more in touch with his feelings than the monk. He knows how to achieve bliss and joy. I hope, though, that after he ate his quart of ice cream he would say, "I love you" to each member of his family. But I didn't tell him that. After all, we know he loves us, so let's let him enjoy his chocolate ice cream. I don't want to rush him because I don't want to be an unenlightened father. If I seem too tough on the monk, forgive me. I need to do more gardening than I want to, and I don't consume much chocolate ice cream.

If you knew you had only fifteen minutes left to live, what would you do? If it is legal and won't harm you or anyone else, do it now, in the next fifteen minutes. Choose your pleasure, what ever your taste.

vi
WORDSWORDSWORDSWORDS

Which is more powerful, the word or the sword?

I FIND LIFE MORE ENJOYABLE when I follow directions literally, the way a naive child would. If a roadside sign says, "No Outlet," I don't take the road unless I have batteries. If the form says, "Sign Here," I sign H-E-R-E. If it says, "Print Your Name," okay, I print Y-O-U-R N-A-M-E. When someone says, "May I say who's calling?" I answer, "Sure, go ahead." If the sign says, "Don't Throw Foreign Objects in the Toilet," I report dropping something from Italy in the bowl. I especially enjoy trying out baby changing shelves, although our grandchildren don't seem any different no matter how many times I put them on one.

One night Bobbie and I and our four cats were driving home from Florida after visiting our son Stephen and his family, and we stopped at a truck stop at three A.M. As we entered the large dining area, I could see many tired truck drivers slumped over tables and counters. In the doorway a large homemade sign read, "Wet Floor." I walked up to the sign and said in a loud voice to the waitress, "Do I do this before or after I eat?"

The waitress stopped in her tracks, and all the drivers sat bolt upright to see what kind of lunatic had just come in. When they saw Bobbie's smile they knew I was harmless and had not been let out on my own. We had a great time now that everyone was awake, and we got good service, too. Waitresses have to be careful; you never know whether a customer is serious or not.

The other day I was filling out a form in a physician's office and I came to an item asking whether I have female problems. I checked "Yes." I was serious about that one. After all, I am a married man.

The best kinds of directions to follow carefully and precisely are the ones only you can see and hear, but that's another story, about the wisdom of your inner voice.

One day many years ago our son Stephen brought home a painting he had done on which he had written "words" over the entire canvass. It said, "WORDSWORDSWORDSWORDS."

The words became swords, a fact that fascinated me. I hung the picture up and from time to time I look at it and think about the power of words and swords. Both can be used to injure or to heal. A scalpel can wound a vital organ or it can drain an abscess. A cruel word can destroy a life, and a kind word can heal one.

Stephen's visual combination of words and swords fascinated me because I use both in my professional life. I started as a surgeon, which I think was a way of making up for damage I did with a sword in a past life. As a surgeon, I used a knife to cut away people's afflictions. But when my patients taught me how powerful words could be, I also began to use the spoken and written word to help people heal themselves and live more fully.

Which has been the more powerful tool? When I was starting out as a surgeon I'm sure I would have said the sword, but today I have to say the word has been more powerful in my life. The number of people I have helped with the sword is in the thousands. But my words are at work in nineteen languages and in the homes of millions of people. I receive mail from places I will never get to in this lifetime and people I will never meet and certainly never operate on. So here is one vote for the word being more powerful than the sword.

A patient once gave me a Quaker calendar that illustrated the power of words. The calendar shared the story of a man who traveled fewer miles—by far—in his life than I travel in a year. He spent his entire career working in an area roughly the size of my home state of Connecticut. He had a small circle of friends, and the crowds that attended his lectures and seminars were small by today's standards. Yet this man's words had the power to change the world.

His name was Jesus. I am not in his class, though we have the same father. You and I may not be prophets, but our words can be as powerful as the words of prophets, mahatmas, gurus, clergy and philosophers. We have within us the ability to heal the sick, help the blind to see and the crippled to walk. If we speak His words, if we speak of hope, love and faith, there is no telling what we can accomplish with our wordswordswords.

vii
The Wisdom of the Ages

Create something

I WALKED INTO A COFFEE SHOP on Cape Cod and saw a sign that said, "Order Here." I told the waitress to wash my car, vacuum our living room rug and then shop for us. She didn't do a single thing I ordered her to do.

Later that day when we were out driving I saw a sign that said, "Wildlife Refuge." At last. Just what I needed! I headed straight for the refuge. Finally, a chance for me to live wild, free of inhibitions and restrictions, free to just be my abnormal self. Well, it turned out to be another disappointment. The rangers wouldn't let me move into the refuge because I was domesticated and not endangered, sick or injured, and I had no fur or feathers.

Not long after, I saw a bag in the pet store labeled, "Wild Bird Seed." I bought the bag and could hardly wait to get it home. It was another disappointment. The seeds were as tame and well behaved as the seeds I usually buy. I tried planting the seeds, but I couldn't grow a single wild bird.

Very little, in my experience, is what it claims to be.

One of our sons and his wife opened a store in Simsbury, Connecticut, called The Wisdom of the Ages. This store is what it claims to be. People can just walk in and buy all sorts of things they need to live their lives more fully: spiritual messages about love and health, crystals, jewelry, T-shirts, books, pictures, toys for the children. The store offers massage therapy and a variety of goods and services to help you enjoy life, get in touch with the wisdom of the ages and heal.

Of course you do not have to go shopping for the wisdom of the ages. It is available in the sacred texts of your own spiritual tradition. You can find it there for free and pass it on to your children. They are not too young for it, because wisdom is not necessarily related to age. I know children whose life experiences have made them wiser than most adults. Some people do gain wisdom with their years, but many do not, and what older folks teach is not necessarily right or true.

If you don't read religious texts and you are not shopping in Simsbury, where can you find the wisdom of the ages? This is a seek-and-learn process. Wisdom is universal and in harmony with the nature of life. It is not trapped by the rules and regulations of organized religion, which, sadly, sometimes separate us. If you have wisdom and know what you are doing, you do not have to question your activities. You could, for instance, work on the Sabbath without doing any harm, as Jesus and his disciples knew. The Sabbath is set aside as a day of rest, but if your activities are in harmony with the nature of life you are not working but creating, and creation is the job we were sent here to do. Love and compassion do not divide us.

This is the best summary I know about the wisdom of the ages: Go forth and create. As you create, be kind, compassionate and unattached to the results.

Creating is easy if you view the world as if you were a child. Playing and creating are almost synonymous. Personally, I like playing with words and using them to turn things upside down. I like talking to strangers and making deals with children in airports. That type of play may not appeal to you. You must find your own way to play and lose track of time and discover the wisdom of the ages.

This is your creation prescription: Choose one dose, every day, beginning today. Make up a song. Repair something. Plant

some flowers. Build a climber for your cats. This prescription
should be followed faithfully. Every single day, it is critical that
you create something. You decide what it will be.

viii

"You Can't Use Conversations with God"

How to hear the voice of God

WHILE SPEAKING TO A LARGE AUDIENCE one evening, I announced I
was going to write a book called *Conversations with God*. After my
talk, a young woman came up and said, "You can't use that title.
My father already wrote a book called *Conversations with God*."

Her father, Neale Walsh, has indeed written a wonderful
book about his conversations with God. When I told God, in
our next conversation, that my title was used, She said, "Then
call your book *From God Knows Where*."

When I talk about my conversations with God, am I being
metaphorical? Not entirely. Yes, I do embellish by giving God
human traits in the stories I tell about Her. But I am serious
about the Creator speaking to us. It happens, and a lot more
often than we realize. I do hear voices.

Sometimes it is best not to let others know you hear God's
voice. As Lily Tomlin points out, when you talk to God, it's
called prayer; when God talks to you, it's called schizophrenia.

Suppose you do hear a voice. Suppose you are out walking
and you hear a voice speaking to you, and the words are perfectly clear and sensible and helpful. Where are they coming

from? Bobbie says, "God only knows." I say, "From God knows where." I offer these as specific answers, not evasions.

Some would suggest that the voice comes from my unconscious. I won't argue the point, but I will remind you that the Bible tells us that in the beginning, there was the word, and the word was with God, and the word was God. If God is consciousness, why shouldn't we be able to be aware of what God is thinking? We are a part of that consciousness. We are a part of creation. Why wouldn't we hear the words of our Creator and know His thoughts?

But we don't hear God's words all the time, and some of us may never hear them. Why? I know several reasons you might not hear the voice of God. You might have five children, as Bobbie and I did, and your children may make a lot of noise and you may be distracted by work, fatigue, fear and worry. That deafened me for many years. Or you may have your antenna directed toward other stations and be listening to the other programs. God's voice may be drowned out by the sounds that surround you—sounds of the city or your work. Even the sounds of nature can distract you and make you miss the voice when it speaks.

I think our Creator surrounded us with many sounds and languages in the hope that we would focus on one universal voice common to us all. That hasn't worked too well, but you can't blame the Creator. She gave us free will, and it is our choice to listen to the babble around us rather than Her voice.

You can help yourself hear God by creating harmony and rhythm in your life. This does not mean you need silence. It means you have to find your song, and you have to surround yourself with sounds that are part of your rhythm. Different people have different songs: some might find theirs in a machine shop, others in the woods, others shut alone in their study. Engine noises or the rustling of the leaves or the ticking of a clock or silence will distract some of us but will be part of the orchestration for others.

If you find your own harmonious way and listen carefully, you will hear the voice of God. It is always available, but the sounds may be very subtle. God leaves it to us to set our antennae in the right direction, be still and listen.

Remember the parable of the satellite dish, remote control and television set. You are capable of receiving many stations that carry many messages and voices—more even than the hundred channels now available in many areas. You also have a remote control device, your mind, which allows you to select what you see and hear. Your body is the screen that displays the signal you have selected. If you have decided to tune into the Word of God, you will be a co-creator, and your life and your activities will bring meaning and compassion into the world.

Men, in particular, need to remember to stop channel hopping and to focus on the most important message they can hear: a message of love for all of creation. Tuned in to that message, we can create a true garden of Eden.

Scientists tell us the universe began with a big bang. Is that a metaphor, or was there really an explosion of sound at the moment of creation? We have no way of knowing, but personally I don't think everything started with a loud sound.

I prefer to think that creation began with a sound I once heard when Bobbie and I were riding on a bike trail over the sand dunes on Cape Cod. We stopped to rest in a sheltered spot where there was no wind, no sound of cars or machines or insects or birds. There were no sounds at all. Just silence. The silence was so loud it was overwhelming, and I got back on my bike and started riding to create sounds again.

This happened years ago. If I am lucky enough to hear that silence again today, I will not be so quick to get away from it.

Now I know that silence is the sound of creation. In complete silence, you can hear the Creator at work.

Artists know how to tune in to the voice of creation. When they are ready to create, they go into their workplace and wait. Many have routines or rituals they go through to clear their minds and to open themselves while they are waiting. What are they waiting and preparing for? The voice that tells them what words to write or what colors to use.

When we stop worrying and hurrying and prepare ourselves to listen we can begin to hear. I hear the voice when I go out each morning to be alone with myself. I jog or bicycle, but you can walk or even drive a car and hear the voice. The key is to find a rhythm, to be calm and silent inside and to stop filling your mind with your own words. The words you hear then will come from some other source. They will speak to you about yourself and your life, and they will reveal that you are surrounded by wisdom that is always available and that is always within you.

You may want to carry a pad and pencil or tape recorder to write down or record the words of wisdom so you don't forget them by the time you get home. It may seem odd that you would forget messages from God, but we forget Her words as easily as we forget dreams, so it helps to write them down.

ix

Creation Began with a Big Band

More ways to hear the voice of God

THE OTHER DAY I WAS SITTING IN SILENCE listening to the tick of a clock. Sixty seconds each minute. I felt calm and peaceful listening to the clock, and I started thinking about the whole notion of seconds, and why there are sixty seconds in a minute. Why not one hundred? Who came up with the seconds, and why? As I listened to the tick, tock, I noticed how calming it is, like the slow, steady pulse of a distance runner.

I know from my experience as a surgeon that music and rhythm have a big effect on people. I relied on both to calm and focus staff and patients in the operating room. Sixty seconds and sixty minutes are healing rhythms. If we listen to those rhythms, we stop hurrying. On the other hand, I have a pendulum clock that ticks twice every second, once as it swings up and once as it swings back. That clock rushes me, tells me to hurry, to move along and get the work done, and then every fifteen minutes it makes a loud chime to remind me to hurry up, move it, time is passing.

While I was writing about silence and explosions and the moment of creation, I made an interesting typing error. I wrote "big band" instead of "big bang." I'd like to think that was not an error but the voice of creation typing for me. From now on, that's my theory on the origin of everything: Creation began with a big band, and ever since there has been rhythm, style and beauty throughout the universe. Our job is to look and listen for the big song, and then to join in, following the beat established by the conductor leading the big band.

Where do we find the conductor? How do we tune in to Her voice and Her message? One obvious way is through meditation or prayer. There are many books or tapes that can teach you the techniques, if you don't already know how. There are no great secrets here, but you have to take the first step of setting aside the time to do it.

You may find it hard to set aside time to listen. Fortunately, God has a way of getting through to us when we are too busy or too distracted to let Her get a word in edgewise: She speaks to us in our sleep.

Carl Jung titled his autobiography *Memories, Dreams, Reflections*. He knew that the reflections we see in memories and dreams are mirrors that reveal us to ourselves. I think the Creator chose to communicate with us through dreams and visions because She knew fewer miscommunications occur when you use images. We can play with words. We can lie with language and deceive ourselves and one another. What we see when we look at other people and in the mirror or in our dreams is more direct and honest. There are foreign languages but no foreign images. Yes, we can argue about the meaning of images or symbols just like we argue over the meaning of words, but when we experience the powerful images that come in dreams we understand them on a level deeper than words.

When you study myths and images you begin to see how similar our symbols are around the world. Elisabeth Kübler-Ross once told me she could travel all over the world with a box of crayons and make sense of the drawings done by people in every culture. No matter what culture we are raised in, our dreams and symbols come from the same source. Some have been with us since our creation and some are part of our common human history.

When you think about how busy we are not listening during our waking hours, you can appreciate how wise God is to use our sleeping time to communicate with us. This is the one time when we are quiet and there are no distractions and our remote control is turned off. God built us in such a way that when we sleep, our remote control devices slip from our hands and our receivers automatically turn to Her channel and receive Her message. Our eyes and ears are receiving even when we are in a coma, asleep or anesthetized.

Of course, we can refuse to rest even when we are exhausted. We can spend our nights restlessly worrying about tomorrow and we can refuse to pay attention to the messages God sends in our dreams. Then God has to resort to other ways to gain our attention. But I'd rather watch the signs God puts before me each day and night than have to be hit over the head by a disaster because I wasn't paying attention.

> *This is a prescription you cannot fill until you go to bed. Tonight I want you to tune in to the Really Big Show. Go to sleep. Dream. Wake and write down all the images you can remember. Now you have messages from God that you can meditate on. If you need help figuring out what the images in your dreams mean, there are a number of good books to help you. Jung is a marvelous guide, but remember that within the dream there is personal as well as universal meaning. Some universal symbols have significance for all of us, but there also will be very specific messages attached to those symbols. Remember also that dreams often are not to be taken literally. They most often are metaphors. You have to figure out what the people and events in the dream represent for you.*

x
Love Is Blind

How to see the face of God

I ONCE STUMPED MY PHILOSOPHY TEACHER by asking, "If love is blind, why did St. Augustine say we must love in order to see?" He didn't give me any answer.

The answer, I think now, is this: True love is not really blind; it is, in fact, a way of seeing. It is blind only in the sense that the lover does not focus on the loved one's flaws or shortcomings.

But the true lover has vision because he or she is open to all that is present. The lover sees with heart and not just head.

Do not be afraid to love. Remember dear old Don Quixote, viewing the world with love. He saw many beautiful things no one else saw. Try being dear Don Quixote for a day. You'll see that love improves your vision and allows you to see more than your eye has ever seen before. But be forewarned: Those who look on the world with love will need a handkerchief, not to use as a blindfold, but to blow their nose and dry their tears.

There is another technique that can help you see what is really going on. I am not talking about seeing subversive activities or plots. I am talking about seeing all the beauty in the world that usually goes unobserved. The technique for seeing glorious sights is simple: Create a work of art.

When I was in emotional turmoil because of the difficulties of being a physician, I found great healing in painting. Creating pictures healed my body and brought me peace of mind. As I painted, I lost track of time and any sense of physical or emotional distress. But something else happened, too. In order to paint a portrait, I had to learn what the person or object in the painting really looked like. I had to start looking more closely than ever at the colors, shapes, shadows and highlights of life. Painting made me aware of things I had never seen before, even though they were in front of me every day of my life.

Later I learned that painting is not the only art that improves your vision. When I began to write, I discovered that although I could now see the world well enough to paint a portrait or a scene, I could not describe the world's beauty in words. Again, I had to learn how to see things I had been looking at all my life and translate them into words.

It is not important whether anyone ever reads my stories

or sees my paintings. The writing and painting taught me to see a different world, and that new vision enhanced my life. I feel at times like an extraterrestrial who has just set foot on the planet and is seeing everything for the first time. Try looking at the world this way. The next time your window is covered by frost, don't get angry as I did one day. Study the ice crystals. See their beauty. Examine their elegance of form. Rejoice in creation's artwork. Then write a poem about it or paint a picture of it and store it in your art gallery of life. Remember, your artwork is not going to be graded. It is a fine creation whatever it looks or sounds like, and it belongs on display.

I spend a lot of time standing in front of audiences or sitting in airports, and I get to see an amazing number of faces. The most remarkable thing about many thousands of faces I see every year is the variety. I know from being a surgeon that our interiors are all the same basic color and design, but I see from being a face watcher that our exterior features are remarkably varied. I'm not sure why God made our interiors so similar (it couldn't be just to make life easier for surgeons), but I think I know why She made our exteriors so different.

Imagine if we all looked alike. Imagine if we had only one variety of fruit, vegetable, flower, tree, insect, bird and animal. Pick your favorite of each living plant and creature and imagine a world in which all dogs look alike and the forests and city streets have only elm trees. Creation would be much less interesting if you viewed the same plants and animals and the same faces every day. Watching the bird feeder would not be very exciting. There'd be no point to shopping; you'd just have your food delivered because it would all be the same anyway. A world without variety would diminish our enjoyment and God's reputation.

So remember when you look at the great variety of trees in

the forest or the gallery of faces in the airport, you are looking at the many faces of God.

A prescription to improve your vision: Paint a picture. Or write a poem or story. Better yet, do both. And remember, you don't have to be good at it. You only have to try, because the effort will make you look more closely, and when you look more closely you are guaranteed to see fascinating and beautiful things you have never seen before. Today write a poem about a tree and then paint a picture of a tree. One hint: It's easier when the wind is not blowing.

xi

He Wasn't Coming and He Wasn't Going

Learning what you can and can't control

I READ ABOUT A MONK STANDING ON THE CURB waiting for a ride to the airport. The ride was late, and a neighbor was watching out the window to see if the monk would be picked up in time to make his flight. The neighbor knew he would have been disturbed had he been in the monk's shoes. In fact, as the minutes passed and the ride didn't show up, the neighbor found himself getting anxious. But he noticed the monk was waiting peacefully. "He wasn't coming. He wasn't going. He was just being," the neighbor said.

Just being. It sounds simple, but I admit I struggle every day to just be. It wouldn't be such a challenge if you were sitting in a cave with nowhere to go but into your meditation, but it is hard when you are traveling and trying to stick to a schedule. I think the monk waiting for the ride must have known the difference between order and control.

You cannot control everything, no matter how much you try, or worry, or brood. But if you work at it, you can keep your thoughts in order. The monk couldn't control what time his ride arrived, but he could control what was in his mind as he waited. When you control your thoughts, you maintain order in your mind, body and soul. With order in your mind, you can live a life of order no matter what is happening around you or even to you.

Having ordered thoughts and an ordered life brings a sense of peace and even, in an indirect way, a sense of control. When your life is in order, you enter into the universe's schedule and you have fewer problems being on time. Before I go out for speaking engagements, I send a list of requirements. I always write on the list, "Don't worry, I will take care of the weather." Most people think that's a joke, but I think it is possible our thoughts do affect the weather, and I've heard of rainmakers and quantum physicists who would not find the connection preposterous.

Carl Jung met a rainmaker in Africa who told the great psychologist that when he arrives in an area that needs rain he goes into a tent to separate himself from the unhealthy consciousness of the local inhabitants. He then meditates to restore a healthy consciousness, and it rains. Reading about that rainmaker was what inspired me to put the weather on the list of things I take care of when I travel. Sometimes I bring rain to areas of drought. Other times I bring sunshine. I have not yet missed a single speaking engagement because of weather since I got on the universe's schedule. I believe that when our work is in harmony with nature, we help bring life what it needs to survive.

. . .

At some conferences the organizers hold up signs for speakers showing exactly how much time they have left. This strikes me as a bit compulsive, but I understand they just want everything to run on schedule. Some of the signs have numbers (10 or 5 or 2) and some say simply, "TIME"—meaning, "That's it. Your time is up."

I took the "TIME" sign home from one lecture, and now I carry it with me and hold it up for the audience when I lecture. "That's it," I tell them. "Time is all you have. Be aware of your time and use it wisely."

You are truly on schedule only when you are using your time to give love to others. This doesn't mean you have to be a doormat and do whatever anyone asks you to do. Being on schedule means finding your heart-time zone. When you are in that zone, you feel right about your life, and then your time is never wasted. If you are giving love in your way, then your life is joyous. When someone holds up the "TIME" sign you will come off the stage feeling that you did what needed to be done and said what needed to be said.

I know the feeling of wanting to go back on stage or wanting to add a few pages to a book because I remembered something important after the "TIME" sign went up. But when you speak from your heart, this does not happen. Your heart knows what needs to be said in the time you have.

One day I was speaking in a synagogue where there were no clocks in the sanctuary. The rabbi asked me to speak for eighteen minutes, because eighteen in Hebrew is Chai, which is also the word for "life." He asked if I wanted a signal to alert me when my eighteen minutes were almost up. I felt I was in my heart zone that day so I told him I would not need any reminders, and I would speak for eighteen minutes. I delivered my sermon and stopped without any signal, and as I came down from the pulpit the rabbi whispered, "You spoke exactly eighteen minutes"—which I already knew, because that day I was not coming or going, not worrying or calculating. I was just being and speaking from my heart.

xii
Is Your Go-Round Merry?

Choose the ride that's right for you

ONE JULY MORNING I woke up with vertigo. The room started spinning as soon as I stood up. So I sat back down. The symptom said to me, "Your world is spinning around. Go back to bed. Get some rest." The vertigo, I realized, was a warning that I'd depleted my body by training too hard in the heat of summer for the New York City Marathon. So I took my body's advice and rested and replaced the depleted fluids.

While I was resting I thought about the spinning sensation and remembered carnival rides I'd taken as a kid. I spent a minute thinking about the different rides and how they are like life. Are our lives a merry-go-round? We have to stop and ask ourselves, Am I just going around in circles making myself dizzy? That morning my body told me to get off the ride and rest a while and not get back on until my head stopped spinning. I am the driver. I can determine the speed at which I go around.

You may find merry-go-rounds tame. Perhaps your life is more like a roller coaster ride. That's okay, as long as it is the ride you want to be on. Maybe you enjoy the highs and lows of the roller coaster. I have fun on the merry-go-round, where I can meet people of all ages and we can talk while we ride. The kind of conversations and interactions I like are impossible when we are alternately shrieking or tense with anticipation. But if that kind of life is truly your choice and makes you happy, then go ahead and ride the roller coaster.

Whatever ride you choose in the carnival of life, just remember to stop, now and then, for a rest and refreshments. And those of us who are carousel riders should definitely take a break whenever the merry drops out of the merry-go-round.

3
Loving Yourself

i
"I'd Never Expose My Dogs to Smoke"

How to tell if you are being good enough to yourself

ON A RECENT VISIT to our son Stephen's family in Florida, we went into a supermarket to buy groceries. While the young woman at the cash register scanned and bagged our purchases, she asked, "How are you tonight, sir?"

"Depressed," I answered. "I ran out of my medication and my therapist is away, so I can't renew my prescription."

"I know how you feel. I'm not doing so well, either," she said. "My boyfriend is very spiritual and he is mad at me."

As she continued to scan and bag our groceries, the young woman explained that her boyfriend was upset with her because she smoked. I said, "You are a child of God; why don't you love yourself enough to stop smoking?"

"If I were pregnant, if I had a child in me, I'd stop."

"Why can't you love yourself as much as a baby?" I asked. "You were a beautiful baby once. Picture this; your dog comes in the door with a cigarette dangling from his lips. I'll bet you'd say, 'Put that out and don't let me see you doing that again.'"

She smiled and said, "We have two dogs at home. My mother and I smoke outside so we don't expose them to the smoke."

Later on the same visit, I was sitting at a table in a small delicatessen with Stephen and his wife, Marcia. The waiter went by three times with the same sandwich on a tray. I asked why he was walking around with the same sandwich and he said, "I can't find who ordered it and I don't know what to do with it."

"Give it to me," I told him. "I'll take it home and feed it to Stephen's dogs."

The waiter wrapped the sandwich up and we took it home. When I started to unwrap it for the dogs, Stephen noticed the kind of meat it contained.

"You can't feed that meat to the dogs. It isn't good for them," he told me, as he took the sandwich out of my hands and put it in the refrigerator. You know the rest of the story. Later on that afternoon, Stephen was munching away on the sandwich that wasn't good enough for the dogs.

My response to the young woman smoking on the porch and to our son eating the meat-filled sandwich is the same: "I hope someday you will love yourself as much as you love your dogs."

You can find examples of how little we value ourselves everywhere you look. The signs on the front of the convenience stores where Stephen lives in Florida tell the story. Beer, ice, bread and milk are the big come-ons. The order of the words varies, but beer and ice are always two of the top four staples for sale. If we were all taking care of ourselves, wouldn't the convenience stores compete for our dollars with signs that read, "Fruit, Vegetables, Bread, Milk"?

If you love yourself, you take good care of yourself. But early in life many of us, usually due to poor parenting, stop loving ourselves and lose a sense of our own value. Others grow up with a sense of self-worth but get beaten down by the difficulties of life and then give up caring about themselves. I don't want to criticize people and tell them what to do. But I would like to see everyone accept themselves and love themselves as much as they love their pets.

Some people only learn to love themselves when a life-threatening illness awakens them. When they are facing death, they stop smoking and start eating fruits and vegetables. Why wait until your life is almost over to realize that you should care for yourself as well as you care for your favorite pet?

ii

The Ugly Duckling

Something to reflect upon

I PROBABLY TALK ABOUT THE IMPORTANCE OF LOVING yourself almost as much as I talk about the importance of loving other people. I am not encouraging people to be self-indulgent and focused only on themselves. You must love other people to have a truly fulfilling life, but you have to start by loving yourself. If you hate yourself and neglect yourself, what are you going to do when someone comes along and advises you to love your neighbor as you love yourself?

If you have trouble loving yourself, think about the ugly duckling. Remember how the little foundling embarrassed his mother and his siblings by being different? How his mother was constantly explaining or making excuses to the neighbors for his behavior and his looks? Then one day, tired of making excuses, she cast him out of the nest.

The ugly duckling wandered about the world, alone and forlorn, until at last he met kindred spirits who gave him the gift of reflection. Encouraged, the duckling looked into the still water of a pond and saw for himself the truth his duckling family hadn't seen—that he was a beautiful swan.

In life, the mirror-holder often turns out to be someone outside the family. I held the mirror for Stewart, a chubby boy who attended a camp where I was a counselor before I went to medical school. Every afternoon the counselors chose teams by alternating picks—an effective way of balancing out the talent but an excruciating experience for the kids who are not picked until the end.

Having had some experience as an ugly duckling myself, I saw how badly it hurt Stewart to be passed over round after round. I decided there were better things I could do with my picks than choose a winning softball team. One afternoon I made Stewart my first pick. When I saw how happy it made him, I decided to pick another clumsy camper on the next round, and another the round after that. Before long all the really clumsy kids and poor athletes were gathered around me and I was forced to start choosing some who were only mediocre.

Did my team win that afternoon? No. Did we have fun? Yes. We had more fun before we took the field than our opponents had all afternoon.

The next day I chose Stewart first again and continued to choose someone unlikely on every round. Same thing the next day and the day after. By the end of the week, a group of ugly ducklings had stopped dreading the choosing-up ritual and had started looking forward to our afternoon games. No longer outcasts, they started thinking of themselves as my regulars, and though we never won a game, we had spirit. We were a team and loved playing together.

At the end of the two-week session Stewart brought his parents over to meet me. They said with surprise that for the first time, he actually seemed to have enjoyed camp that year, and they were very pleased. I didn't tell them what had made the difference. I met a lot of surprised parents that summer, parents who had dropped off ugly ducklings and were picking up swans.

We are all unborn swans, and have within us the power to be swans and to create swans. A caring schoolteacher or a physician who is unafraid of showing unconditional love can be a mirror in which students or patients discover their own beauty. I've had patients call me asking for Jack Kevorkian's phone number. When they learned they were swans, they found self-love, repaired relationships and cured their diseases.

My own ugly duckling experience came early in life. My mother was two weeks overdue, and after two days of labor, a difficult forceps delivery was performed. According to my mother, I entered the world bruised and ugly, with a purple melon for a head. She was embarrassed by my appearance and could not immediately accept me or show me to anyone. Fortunately I was not cast out of the nest. I had something Hans Christian Andersen's duckling didn't have. I had a loving grandmother whose ability to love was not tempered by how I looked.

My mother's mother anointed my head with oil and massaged my features many times a day. She pushed things back into place until I looked like a reasonably normal infant. There aren't any before and after pictures, which proves my point. No one wanted a picture of me. I don't know how much she really changed my appearance or how much her uncritical acceptance gave my mother the courage to love an ungainly infant. I know my grandmother's touch gave me the warmth, love and physical closeness I needed until my mother could take over.

I had my grandmother. Stewart had me. The duckling had the swans. But you do not need anyone else to save you. You do not have to spend the winter hiding in the reeds waiting for someone to come along and point out your beauty. You can turn yourself into a swan because you have a wonderful mirror you can hold up for yourself.

Remember the one thing that reminds everyone how promising each human life is? Think of the audiences sighing at the babies I hold up. It works every time, and it will work when you do it for yourself, too. Your own baby pictures can be your mirror. If you get them out and look at them now, I guarantee you will see a young swan. Now go and reflect upon your beauty.

Here is a prescription for the affliction of self-esteem depletion. Carry your own baby pictures in your wallet. Take them out every day and look at them in admiration. They will remind you to be as good to yourself as you are to your pets. Put your baby picture up where you work. People will be kinder and less critical when they admire the beautiful baby and learn it is you. And if you put it on your driver's license you will rarely get a ticket for speeding.

iii

A Wedding Night Story

There's only one right answer when you have to make a difficult decision

WHEN OUR WEDDING RECEPTION WAS OVER I borrowed my father's car and set out with Bobbie for Cape Cod. We had a few dollars from wedding gifts given to us that day, and we planned to honeymoon on the Cape until the money ran out. It didn't look like the money would last long, but that didn't turn out to be our biggest problem.

The wedding party was held at a New York City hotel, and we left too late to make it all the way to the Cape that night. We pulled off Exit 66 on the Merritt Parkway at about nine o'clock that night to look for a motel. We drove around Wallingford, Connecticut, until we found a reasonable-looking motel. Later that night the roar of a freight train revealed that a railroad track ran right behind our honeymoon motel, but that didn't turn out to be our biggest problem.

By the time we checked in it was quite late. But that didn't turn out to be our biggest problem, either. When we told the restaurant staff that it was our wedding night, they let us into the restaurant and fixed us turkey sandwiches. Now every time we drive past Exit 66 we acknowledge the Yankee Silversmith Inn and our first meal.

After we unpacked and settled in our room, I told Bobbie I would use the bathroom first and make myself as handsome and fragrant as possible. An hour later when I came out of the bathroom my wife was gone. Now you know my biggest problem.

Bobbie was gone, but sitting on the bed was a giant frog. I love animals, so I figured I had nothing to lose by asking the frog, "Do you know where my wife is?"

The frog answered, "It's me."

"What do you mean, 'It's me'?"

"It's me, Bobbie. Your wife. A spell was cast on me many years ago. For twelve hours I'm a beautiful woman and for twelve hours I'm a frog. I was going to tell you about this before I changed, but you were in the bathroom so long that midnight passed and I changed. Since I didn't have time to warn you, I'll let you decide what schedule I should follow from now on. When should I be a woman and when should I be a frog?"

Now my biggest problem was bigger. How could I decide what was best for myself and for my wife, whom I loved? I could choose for her to be beautiful during the day and she'd impress the neighbors, but then I'd have to sleep with a frog. The other choice would make for pleasant nights but bizarre days. And who would make dinner? The longer I sat the harder the decision became. Then I remembered the wonderful way my mother answered questions when a decision needed to be made.

My mother told me that my father lost his job shortly after they were married, which confirmed her parents' opinion of him. He would go and sit in the unemployment office every day waiting for a job offer. He was only required to check in, but he would spend the day there because that way my mother's parents thought he had gone to work and didn't know he had lost his job. One day he called my mother from the unemployment office. "Rose, I have two job offers. One is a civil service job that is secure but without much chance for advancement, and the other is Paramount Theaters, which is insecure but I could advance. Which one should I take, Rose?"

What do you tell your spouse in such a situation? There is only one right answer, and my mother knew it. "Si," she said, "do what will make you happy." He answered "I feel I should take the Paramount offer," not "I think," and did what felt right for him.

My mother's wisdom saved my marriage because I realized her answer was the answer I should give the frog. I mean my wife. I said, "Frog, I mean honey, do what will make you happy. Make your own schedule and I will be happy to live with it."

The frog said, "Your generosity has freed me from the

spell. I can now be a beautiful woman all the time." She has been ever since, and her face is a treasure.

Think about a big decision you made recently. Think about what your alternatives were. Which would have made you happiest? Which did you choose? Why?

Reflect on other big decisions you have made and try to figure out why you made the choices you made. What criteria do you use in making important decisions? Do you choose the alternative that seems most responsible? That will prove something to someone? To yourself? That will make someone else happy? Try to state your decision-making strategy as concisely as Rose's advice to Si. Do your decisions come from your head or your heart? Mind or body?

Now think about a decision you think you may have to make soon. If you know what your options will be, don't just think about them but ask yourself: Which of the alternatives will make me happy, and how do I feel about them?

iv
Site to Be Developed

What can you make of yourself with the material available?

"SITE TO BE DEVELOPED." When you see this sign you know someone is preparing to put up a building of some kind. It may be an improvement over what currently exists on the site, or it may do more damage than good. We have all seen nature destroyed in the name of development.

Think of yourself as a site to be developed. Remember that different sites are suited for different types of development. What is your goal? What resources are available, and what will best fit your site? Look yourself over and get a feeling for your site. Ask for help from developers and landscapers. Then begin construction. Don't worry about what the sidewalk supervisors think about the structure you are building. This structure is going up on your property and you decide what it will be, or you will find no joy in the life you construct. It will be someone else's building and you will be stuck in it.

A project under development. An ugly duckling. A white canvas or a hunk of potter's clay. I offer metaphors to remind you that you can change yourself and create a more fulfilling life—if you remember my mother's advice to make the decisions that will make you happy. You can create and re-create. This is not about selfishness, but about authenticity.

How much can you do with yourself? No one knows. I know you can be happy. You can be loving. You can take part in creation and live and work in your heart zone. There are no limits. What will happen then? No one knows the details, but I do know you will have what you need, peace and joy.

I said earlier that time doesn't pass and you don't age while you are working in your heart zone. Does that mean you could live forever? For two hundred years? I don't know. If we spent every moment of our lives loving and giving, I do believe miraculous things would happen. I don't think our bodies are capable of living forever, but that's not the point. There are communities where people regularly live to be over one hundred. If you study these communities, you find certain similarities. Yes, of course they exercise and eat reasonable diets. But they also feel useful as they age. These communities value older people and rely on them for taking care of children or other work. As they grow older, people still have meaning in their lives so they go on living. In these communities when people lie about their age, they claim to be older than they are because their age is something for them to be proud of. They are not like my mother-in-law, who at ninety-five said, "My age is not a matter for discussion."

If we want to live long and fulfilling lives, we need to make our communities more like those mentioned above. Meanwhile, we can try to live as much as possible in our own heart zone, the healthiest neighborhood and the place where we are giving love in our unique way. When we are working in our heart zone, we have no awareness of time, are fully alive and have a healthy, youthful, life-enhancing physiology.

What you do in your heart zone depends on who you are. It can be working in the garden, caring for children, writing, building a house, operating on a patient, working in a restaurant or fixing the plumbing. The important thing is that the work has meaning and that you love what you are doing– that will put you in your heart zone. Athletes talk about being in the zone, a state in which they easily, almost effortlessly transcend their usual limitations. When we live in the zone we can transcend the effects of time because we are free of pain and disease in that moment.

It's true you could still die young if you suffer an accident or are poisoned by the environment, but I believe the chances of this are smaller when you are living and loving in your heart zone. Lovers are not invincible, but they do have more resistance to accidents and noxious influences. Relationships have a protective benefit, which is frequently seen in women (who, as a result, live longer than men). "I can't die now," one desperately ill woman told her children. "Not until you're all married and out of the house." And she didn't die for twenty-three years. Another woman who was close to death returned to the hospital after her son's wedding. Everyone expected her to die but she said to her doctor, "Remember, I have another son." And she lived to see him married, too. It's not hormones that make the difference, but desire, attitude and attention.

You can see the protective effect of relationships for men, too. Married men who smoke have less cancer than single men who smoke the same amount. Married men who get cancer live longer than single men with the same cancer. This is not from sleeping with estrogen and progesterone.

If you combine healthy relationships with activities that stop time, who knows how long you are capable of living? There are many stories of people who were threatened with illness and suddenly started living a life of love: Some had their heart disease reversed and some went on to live five years with cancer when it looked like they would be dead in six months. I operated on a landscape gardener who was diagnosed with an incurable cancer in late middle age. He was so busy living, loving and making the world beautiful that the disease disappeared without treatment and he lived into his nineties. Another friend who was a medical student had an "incurable" brain tumor. He is alive today, practicing medicine, with no sign of the tumor. There are many other examples of people with serious illness who lived rich, loving lives and lasted much longer than expected. We know about them and what they are capable of. What we don't know is what we are capable of if we get into a loving state and lose track of time while we are still healthy. The issue is to live in your heart, have magic happen and reap the physical benefits.

v

Candles of Life

Pallbearer or torchbearer

WHY THE EMPHASIS ON LONG LIFE? I ask people at lectures if they want to live to be one hundred. Some say, "Yes, but . . ." And then they qualify their answer: "I only want to live that long if I'm healthy." Others just say yes. I think the second group will live longer, all other things being equal. They are looking forward to life and its opportunities, not worrying about their limitations.

And why not live longer? If you are here to love, you don't need perfect health or a perfect body. You only need time.

Suppose for a minute that a candle ten inches long represents the time you have to live. Do you want to live fully and burn up completely or are you willing to let your flame go out while there are still many inches of candle left? Your candle can still add light and warmth to the world even when it is a stub, but if your behavior is unloving and your lifestyle is unhealthy, you won't achieve your illumination potential.

The length of our candle is probably determined by many factors, including our genes and our environment. But our decisions about how we live determine whether we burn up our entire candle and give off all the light and warmth we were allotted, or extinguish our flame while we still have candle left to burn. We are here to carry a torch. So burn up, not out.

Ask yourself the question I ask at seminars. Do you want to live to be one hundred? If your answer is anything other than an unqualified yes, take out the answers you wrote to the ques-

tions at the end of section vi in the Introduction. What did you decide you are here to accomplish? Whatever you decided to do with your limited time, is it possible you could still be doing it in your seventies? Your eighties? Your nineties? Without a perfect body and with less than perfect health? Now ask yourself again, Do you want to live to be one hundred?

vi
That's Just the Way I Am

The role of nature, nurture and second nature

"I CAN'T HELP IT. That's just the way I am. It's my nature."

These seem to be great excuses and convincing explanations for anything you do. But are they entirely true?

Identical twins raised separately do have amazing similarities in their behavior. Astrologers can sometimes make remarkably accurate predictions about people's behavior based on their birth dates. Nature does play a role in our lives. But identical twins do not always develop the same diseases at the same time. Everyone born with the gene for breast cancer does not develop the disease. Everyone with the gene for obesity is not obese. People born on the same day—even at the same time in the same city—do not live the same life. So clearly there are important factors in addition to our genes and birth signs.

Our biology has a powerful influence over who we are. But our habits also play a role. We develop behavior patterns or personality traits in response to the encouragement, reward, interest or punishment we receive from our parents and other important authority figures who instruct and educate us. We respond like animals in a cage when our behavior is rewarded or punished.

Our physical nature and our habits or patterns of behavior work together to determine the course of our lives. If you have a gene predisposing you to obesity, your life will be very different depending on whether you chose to exercise regularly and eat sensibly or decide to be sedentary and complain about the genes your parents gave you.

The third, and most interesting, influence is our "second nature." Unlike the other two influences, our second nature involves choice. Although we often act out of habit, we are capable of altering our behavior by making choices about how we behave. When we act purposefully rather than habitually, we are creating our second nature. This is why identical twins or people with very similar educations and experiences do not turn out exactly the same. Their lives are different because along the way they make choices and develop their own individualized second nature in response to their experience of life.

Do the things that happen to you influence your second nature? Is it easier, for instance, to develop a healthy second nature if you are loved? Of course. I saw a gifted astrologer accurately pick from a list of birth dates given her which people had turned out to be mass murderers. But the astrologer went on to say, "Perhaps if these people had been loved enough their lives would have been different and they would not have committed such crimes." The point is that love changes people. It is a powerful creative force.

We all have an opportunity and a responsibility to choose whom we would like to be. If we refuse to choose, we run the risk of becoming what we despise in others. Still, it is tempting not to choose, and to let our second nature be shaped by outside or internal influences and forces. It is much harder to do the shaping ourselves, accept responsibility for our behavior and be creative.

Creating a beautiful second nature is difficult because we are human and we each have our own frailties. It is hard to be constructively critical of your own nature. It is much easier to be destructively critical of yourself and others, and then, when people complain, to defend yourself with the old standby: "It's just my nature to be this way." But the truth is, you are capable of changing your nature. Genes and parenting are not the only factors that determine who you are and what happens to you.

One thing you can do to influence your future is to eliminate the things that are killing you. Yes, some of the things that are killing you may be beyond your control. But most of the time when you say, "This or that is killing me," you are talking about things you can do something about, such as your behavior, or responses to a conflicting and difficult relationship or job. It is no coincidence that on Mondays we have more heart attacks, suicides and illnesses.

People say, "I'm downhearted" or "You're breaking my heart." They sing, "My heart cries for you, sighs for you, dies for you." There may be more meaning in those words than we realize. I worry when I hear someone say, "I'll make this marriage work if it kills me." Your marriage may kill you—if you are being abused and beaten. Or you may kill yourself trying to please your spouse or your boss. The things you do to please others or the things you submit to really may be killing you, but you can take action and change your circumstances and save your own life. If something is killing you, eliminate it. That is not the time to be a loving martyr and die trying.

You often can learn about what is killing you from paying attention to the parts of your body that malfunction when you are ill. Your illness is often symbolic, in the sense that your pain or illness tells you what you need to change in your life. It is a metaphor. An obvious example is a headache that feels like pressure or a weight. It tells you that you are under too much stress, or your husband is a burden. Illnesses can point to problems in our lives. A recurrent bladder infection described as a draining experience led a woman to alter what was draining her strength and contributing to her illness. If your backache is a stabbing pain, you might ask yourself if someone in your life is stabbing you in the back. Learn from your body. Don't blame it or yourself.

It is often easier to ignore the signs and go on living the life you happen to be living, even if it is hurting you—right up to the point where you get ill and physical death is a real possibility. Then, when the old distractions and numbing agents aren't doing the trick anymore, you have to make a decision. At that point, some people decide to let their lives kill them, while others decide to make changes in the hope they can enjoy their remaining time. Why wait until you have to make decisions under such pressure?

Make a list of what is killing you and decide what you want to do about it now. Imagine you are talking to someone, and you're saying, "You know what really kills me? . . . " Then answer your rhetorical question. "Our debts. My job. The way we keep arguing over the same things . . ." If you have trouble figuring out what to put on your list, ask your body for a few hints. What is killing your body?

Put the list on the refrigerator with the shopping list and start to work doing something about the things that are killing you.

As you find ways to eliminate problems, cross them off your list. When your "What's killing me" list is empty, start a new list of things you desire to enhance your life, and begin to live.

vii

Multiple Personalities

Finding the interesting characters residing within you

WE EXPERIMENT WITH DIFFERENT PERSONALITIES as children and adolescents to see how our audience responds, but then we tend to stop changing and settle into the safety of one being, one person. The personality we end up with is, for most of us, not one we have freely chosen but one that has been imposed on us. We chose it out of necessity, as a survival mechanism. If you want to be happier and have a more fulfilling, authentic life, you must be willing to begin experimenting again. You cannot change your life and remain the same person. Remember the warning, "He who seeks to save his life will lose it, and he who is willing to lose his life will save it."

You have to be willing to lose your untrue self in order to change and become your true self. Most people do plan to make some changes—later. They say, "When I retire . . . ," "When I have the money . . . ," "When this or that . . ." When people tell me what they are going to do in the future, I respond, "Why don't you start rehearsing and practicing now?"

One woman in her seventies told me her daughter was driving her crazy calling her every day, wanting her to run errands, take care of her cats, water her garden and on and on. I said, "Why don't you say no?"

She said, "I'm not eighty yet. When you get to be eighty, then you can say no."

"I'll tell you what I want you to do," I said. "On Friday, you are to be eighty. Every Friday, you are eighty. You've got to start practicing so when you get to be eighty you'll know how to handle it. For now, you can be seventy-five six days a week but on Fridays you have to be eighty."

You have permission to do the same thing. You can be a kid one or two days a week if that's what you need in order to go fishing for a life. Don't wait for illness, retirement, the lottery or a knock on the head to awaken you. Awaken yourself now. Switch personalities and play your part.

The truth is, we are all multiples anyway, even if we have settled into one comfortable personality. You may be more comfortable hiding your many selves and sticking to your one well-rehearsed role. But the other sides of you are still there. What a shame to force yourself to face every day with the same safe and secure, but inauthentic, personality. You have many talents and you can play multiple roles in the theater of life. When you do try new roles, you will discover wonderful characters residing within you. You don't have to get divorced, change your job and move to another part of the country to have new experiences. You can have all kinds of excitement while you stay married to the same person, keep the same job and live in the same place. You just change personalities, and life remains interesting and exciting. Decide tonight whom you want to be tomorrow, and when you awaken, give birth to your new personality.

viii
Whom Are You Killing?

To whom you are talking when you say, "I hate you?"

YOUNG PEOPLE, MORE OFTEN THAN DISHEARTENED ADULTS, are apt to be thinking about their future and questioning what they might become. Unfortunately, young people are also prone to becoming discouraged when they are not loved, supported or educated, and turn to drugs or attempt suicide to solve their problems.

When I speak to young people I tell them, "It is all right to commit suicide without hurting your body, and to get high without using drugs." When they look puzzled, I tell them it is a mistake to think that the only way to be free of problems is to kill yourself. If you are thinking about suicide, what you need to eliminate is not yourself but the part of your life that is killing you, or making you want to die.

I said you do not need to divorce or change your job to have exciting new life experiences. A change in attitude will work. But you do have to make major changes if you have come to the point where you are considering suicide. If your life is killing you, then children should speak out and seek help. And adults can divorce, quit their jobs or move out. Eliminate what is killing you so you can keep on living. Don't eliminate yourself.

I know a young man who was physically and sexually abused as a child by an HIV-positive adult. Subsequently he developed AIDS. One day he decided to commit suicide by jumping in front of a subway train. God delayed the train, and while the boy was waiting he noticed a sign on the station wall with the telephone number for a suicide hotline. He called and is alive today because his call was answered with love. He has a new life, but he did commit suicide, too. The old life he was living died that day in the subway station.

I asked him why he had decided to kill himself rather than his parents. I said, "You live in New York. You could have gotten a gun." He said, "Because I never wanted to be like them." He was wise enough to realize that killing his parents would not solve his problems. He came close to killing himself, but he discovered that love is what matters; with love he could kill his bitterness and be free to go on living.

How do you get high without using drugs? You can do it by having a near-life experience. You've heard about near-death experiences, but a near-life experience happens when you are doing what you love to do and are totally involved in the task. When it happens, you are altering your mind's perceptions and your body's feelings. With the change in your body's chemistry, you are on a drug high, but the drug is homemade. It was produced in your body. If you are looking for a high, try loving, volunteering, assisting the needy—and then see how it makes you feel. If you have ever rescued an animal you know the feeling of a self-induced high. You cannot experience any pain or disease in this state.

A young woman at one of my workshops stood up and announced she was there to decide whether to commit suicide. I asked her, "What is your favorite animal, and why is it your favorite?" She answered immediately, "An eagle," and went on to give a beautiful description of the grace and beauty of a soaring eagle. Everyone in the room was touched. We could all see that she realized her connection to the eagle. She finished, paused and then announced, "I have decided not to commit suicide."

At other times when I ask people their favorite animal I get very different responses. "I hate pets and I killed my canary," one woman answered. I worried about her because I was afraid she would do the same to herself. She had no self-love, self-worth or self-esteem left.

Life and animals are like mirrors we hold up before us. When you say, "I hate you!," to whom are you speaking? You may have directed the words at someone else, but I believe you are also speaking to a part of yourself when you say, "I hate you." Remember the love lesson: You cannot love another human being unless you love yourself. The same is true of hatred. If you did not hate yourself, you could not truly hate others. I am not talking about anger or righteous indignation. I am talking about what has been stored within you and never expressed. You don't feel deep, bitter hatred for another human being without first feeling that way about yourself and your life. What lives in you will come forth, whether it is love or hate.

With souls there is no normal or abnormal. Each soul is unique, authentic, refreshing and crazy at times. You can't hate something as delightful and spontaneous as another person's soul unless you have already learned to hate your own soul. Yes, there are lost souls who do harm to others, but we can respond to evil acts with compassion and understanding. Our emotional response comes from within us and is related to how we feel when we see our own soul reflected back to us by the mirror of life.

Life is full of painful events, and people who have lost their way and hurt others. Our pain is not lessened when we respond with hatred. In fact, the opposite occurs: When we hate people who hurt us, we come to resemble what we hate, or worse, and then we suffer all the more. What is evil is our response. We have choices, and love is the most powerful elim-inator of all.

The next time you stand in front of a mirror, do an exercise that will, eventually, make it impossible for you to hate other people. Say out loud to your image in the mirror: "I will never hate you. I love you and I will love you until time itself is through." This prescription can heal you more than any other. You will need to practice and rehearse, so start with small areas of yourself. Animals pick it up right away—did you ever see an animal look in a mirror and be concerned with its image? They never say, "I need a shampoo or trim." But you are human, so you will need to work at it. Begin in the right place: with yourself. It's easier to try to change yourself than others.

ix

Let Them Polish Your Mirror

How to become the best you can be

YEARS AGO A PATIENT I was about to discharge from the hospital was giving bottles of liquor to every doctor who had taken care of him—except me. "I'm not giving you one," he told me, "because you were always angry."

"I wasn't angry at you," I explained. "I was angry at the things I had to do to you." Much of my contact with him had involved doing things that hurt—like inserting a tube into his windpipe to force him to cough up secretions.

"I can understand that, but you took it out on me."

Today when I talk to physicians I tell them there is an easy way to know whether they are good doctors. "If your family, patients and nurses criticize you, you are a good doctor."

I didn't always understand this. When I was a young physician, I didn't realize that criticism was a good sign. Now I see that it means people know you care about them and are willing to change. If no one criticizes you, you can take that as a sign that you are perfect, which is unlikely, or that people feel you don't care enough to listen and are not willing to change. No one criticizes a stubborn mule. It doesn't help or change them.

I have been fortunate enough in my life and career to have many good critics. Nurses would hand me lists of ways I could improve, with practical suggestions such as using the intercom rather than bellowing when I needed something. Patients gave me many good suggestions; they asked me to stop frightening them with my serious look and to think in the hallway and smile in their room. My family helped out, too. "You're not in the operating room now," they would tell me when I was too demanding at home.

The Sufi poet Rumi wrote, "Your criticism polishes my mirror." If you understand who you are and respect yourself, you will not see criticism as a problem but as an opportunity to become a better person. When you feel inadequate or imperfect, the criticism is threatening and makes you feel that you have to defend yourself. When you are secure—not perfect, but secure—you can listen to the criticism and consider its value. You can say, "I'm sorry." And "thank you for polishing my mirror," and when it is appropriate you can learn from the criticism and improve your behavior. I say when it is appropriate because there are some people who love to find fault in others. That is their problem.

I wish I had understood the value of simply listening to criticism years ago. I would have had a more peaceful life and would not have allowed myself to become caught up in so much controversy. I certainly would have spent less time on talk shows trying to correct people's views of me and defending my behavior and the ideas I expressed in books and lectures.

I didn't begin to understand how constructive it is to be criticized until the morning the patient told me he was giving everyone but me a bottle of liquor. I listened to his explanation and knew he was right. I had been angry and lacking in compassion. I said, "I'm sorry."

"Then you can have a bottle of liquor, too."

Remember that he was about to be discharged and could have left the hospital without saying a word to me. He took the time to criticize because he saw my pain and reached out to help me.

It is important to accept criticism and learn from it, but that does not mean you should be discouraged by the grades people give you. The worst grade I received in college was a C in creative writing, and I have gone on to write best-sellers. We are all capable of change. We may begin by doing C work and then learn and grow until we are capable of working at a much higher level. The trick is to listen to constructive criticism but not to let the grades you get destroy your confidence—especially when it comes to creative activities. Find teachers and coaches, and practice. That's what all talented people do.

Remember that we are all blank canvases. If you turn in a blank canvas as your work of art you won't receive a good grade. But creation starts when you begin to work, especially if you see the blank canvas as an opportunity to express your talent rather than as a chance to fail. And remember, the canvas is never finished as long as life remains.

When we find our lives flowing in the wrong direction, it is easier to think more about who is to blame and less about how to change course. Think about it. Let's say you board a train, but as soon as it leaves the station you realize it is going in the wrong direction. Do you lash out and blame the train? Or do you recognize your error, get off at the first stop and switch tracks to catch the right train?

It can be tempting to blame others for our loss of direction. We get lots of information about life but little education in life from parents, teachers and other authority figures, who should know better from their experience. Information is about facts. Education is about wisdom and the knowledge of how to love and survive. But no matter how much advice you get, you are the one who chooses which train to board. As you pass through life, pay attention to the signs and stations; if you don't like the scenery, pull the emergency cord and get off the train. There is no other conductor in charge. There is no one who needs to give you permission to transfer. This is your life. Your journey. Your trip to conduct.

One last suggestion about trains: Take a local, enjoy the journey and the stops. When the line ends we will all find ourselves in the same train yard, so why hurry the trip?

If you are considering using prayer to help you find your way, I have some good news: a guarantee that your prayers will be answered.

How can I guarantee something like that? It's easy. When you pray, you are changed. The moment you begin praying, you step into the mystery and become part of it, and you are, inevitably, changed. So your prayers are answered because you are a different person after you pray.

When you embrace the mystery and open yourself to it, a new life is created, resistant to the old problems. You will notice at times that the new life isn't what you asked for. But asking for specific items or for particular events to occur isn't how I define prayer. I cannot guarantee that the orders you place with God will always be filled. Prayer is not a test of God, but a call for help to find your inner strength and talent.

Your prayers for guidance will be answered and provide you with the resources to deal with whatever comes your way. So as you travel, keep the names of your angels on the tip of your tongue and say your prayers. They will be answered in ninety days—guaranteed, or your money back. Having an angel named "Oh shit" helps. Every time I make that exclamation, help arrives.

I was jogging down the road one morning in my usual trance state, singing, "I am strong but Thou art weak," when a voice interrupted to say, "You have the words wrong." I stopped to listen to what I was singing and started laughing. I was about to correct my mistake when the voice spoke again: "Maybe I've done such a good job with you that you're right, and you are strong. Just go ahead and keep singing."

Remember we are all made out of the strong material we sing about. We all have the capability to endure whatever comes our way because we are all made of divine stuff. So keep singing and you will be ready when you get to heaven and a voice asks, "How do you want to be introduced to God?" Then you can just say you are one of the strong ones who doesn't need to be introduced to God. You are made from the same stuff as God and God already knows you.

x

Failure and Humility

Why you needn't fear failure, or how to fail up

I KNOW A YOUNG MILLIONAIRE who feels the money his father gave him ruined his life. He started out with everything and was afraid to try anything because he might fail. He felt compelled to go into business, where he felt he had to be a success. He lived a timid existence and was nagged by the knowledge that he wasn't getting much out of life. He actually was considering suicide. Then he developed cancer. Facing his death, he felt he had nothing to lose so he actually started living. Rather than working in business to accumulate more dollars he didn't need, he spent his time and energy and some of his money studying animals and trying to save them. Today he says that when his body failed him, it saved his life.

What a shame to be so afraid of failure that you stop living. Bobbie has a great one-liner about failure: "Never consider yourself a failure—you can always serve as a bad example." She is right. Failure can be a better teacher than success.

Successful people will tell you that you have to fail many times to succeed at anything at all difficult. Scientists and entrepreneurs will tell you that only amateurs and the inexperienced expect to succeed on their first attempt with one brilliant idea or venture. Professionals with experience know they may generate many failed theories or business ideas before they produce a single useful theory or financial success.

Failure is a great teacher. It is like stirring the earth to prepare it for growth. If you aren't successful yet, it may be because you haven't failed enough times.

But remember: You cannot fail at being yourself. A cat doesn't try to be a tiger, and you shouldn't try to be something you aren't. You are a process, not a product. Your job is to discover what you are and to create that creature. You still won't be perfect, but success isn't about perfection—it is about authenticity. You are a success if you are being your real, authentic self.

You can waste your life being angry and hating your imperfections and failures or you can learn from them. Think of the word "humus," which refers to soil. Humus is also the root word for "humor," "humility" and "humanness." Blemishes are part of nature—yours and mine. If you are in touch with the earth and its qualities—humus and humility, humor and humanness—you can live a life free of guilt, disease and premature death. You will live a life of authenticity, in which your spirit thrives and failure motivates you, and you are free to be challenged by life.

What difference does it make, in the big picture, whether you succeed or fail? Whether you listen to criticism? Whether you are as good to yourself as you are to your dogs? Does it really matter?

Yes, it does. Everything you do makes a difference. Everything you don't do makes a difference, too. If you wave your arm you create a breeze. What does that do to the weather? The effect may be small, but there is an effect, and combined with other small effects it can have a significant effect. Every act we perform has some effect on the choices other people make and the world we live in. We are part of the great puzzle of life, and without us it is not complete.

I carry buttons with me that say, "You Make a Difference." I give them to the people I see acting in a loving way toward other living things. I tell the recipients to scratch their initials on the back and pass it on to someone they see acting out of love. One day you'll get your own button back and realize that we all make a difference in the global climate.

Every act has its effect. To do nothing is an act that stems from feelings of hopelessness and despair. Please remember, no matter how dark the future looks, you can make a difference. When you live the true life you were sent here to live, the difference you make will enhance life rather than destroy it. Do not spend time worrying how big a difference you make. Anything that enhances a life makes a difference: helping one individual recover from a broken heart; easing one person's pain; helping one ugly duckling discover his or her beauty. Keep working as long as you live, and live as long as you can, and when you finish your marathon they will hang a medal around your neck that says, "You Make a Difference."

I was talking to a butterfly and a caterpillar the other day and I asked them what transition is like. I thought the caterpillar might be saddened by having to metamorphose into a butterfly. But the caterpillar told me he didn't see his last caterpillar days as an ending but as a beginning. "When you humans graduate, you don't call it a termination ceremony, you call it a commencement."

The caterpillar is right. Lives end, the sun sets, meals are finished, but we go on with new lives, guided by what we have experienced. There will be pain and loss in our new lives just as there were in our old lives, but we can use what the pain teaches us. Our lives will make a difference in the world. Our job is to be sure that what we contribute enhances life, and to remember that there are no endings but only beginnings.

4
Loving Others

Haven't Got Time for the Pain

Reclaiming your life, thoughts and feelings

OUR HOTEL ROOM WAS ROBBED one evening while we were at dinner. I think I know who did it because on our way down to the restaurant we saw a suspicious-looking man loitering in the hallway near our room. I had a good look at him while we waited for the elevator, and when we returned to our room and found our belongings had been removed, I could picture his face perfectly.

The man took my clothes and a fur coat I bought Bobbie when we were in the Netherlands. He also took jewelry that had been in Bobbie's family for years and was precious to us—and irreplaceable—because of its family history. We reported the theft and gave the police a detailed description of the burglar. Bobbie and I talked about the loss for a while and then went to bed. The next morning, when I tried to do my meditation, I was disturbed by the picture of the man in the hallway and by thoughts of what I would like to do to him. The same thing happened the next morning, and every morning thereafter. Even after we'd checked out of the hotel and returned home, the man's face followed me, and angry thoughts disturbed my morning meditations.

When several weeks had passed and I was still angry over our loss and violation, I realized the burglar was in charge of my thoughts and my life. That morning I decided to reclaim my life and thoughts. I spontaneously visualized the man bringing his children Christmas presents that he purchased with the money he obtained when he sold our possessions. As I pictured the scene, I thought to myself, "If I had known what he was going to do, I would have left a few dollars on the bedside table for him so he could bring his children some really lovely gifts." I finished the visualization smiling, and never again did the man in the hallway trouble my thoughts. Now and then I smile thinking of him and his children.

You can point out that the burglar probably spent the money on drugs rather than his children. Maybe he did. It makes no difference to me what he did with our belongings. I am free because of the change in me. I helped our son Jeff do the same thing when his home was robbed, only this time the robber bought his mother a birthday present. Now Jeff laughs about the incident and my irrational thinking. But it works.

I was listening on the car radio to Carly Simon singing, "I Haven't Got Time for the Pain." There is wisdom in that song. Our time here is limited. We don't have the luxury of extra time to spend in pain. Some pain may be necessary—for instance, the pain that protects you from an injury or leads you to respond to the needs of others. But the pain you feel when something or someone is disturbing your life and thoughts is not useful, and you will be happier when you resolve the problem and reclaim your life.

The burglar taught me that events are not my problem. My thoughts about the events are the problem. This is fortunate, because I can't change the things that have happened but I can change my thoughts about them.

What thoughts are so important that it is worth holding on to them even when they make you miserable? Why are you holding on? You are in charge of your thoughts and feelings. If you are willing to search for the reason that you can't let go of disturbing thoughts, you can learn about yourself and restore your own peace of mind.

If something controls you in a way that puzzles you, think of it as a mystery. Mysteries are best approached by closing your eyes and mouth to experience darkness and silence. I find new and healing images in that dark, silent place away from emotions that control me. Do not be afraid to close your eyes and be silent in prayer, meditation, rest or sleep. In those states you may rediscover a new self. Then your life, time and thoughts will become yours again and you can live your unique myth.

You are in charge of your visions, images and feelings, and you can transform the ones that disturb you. What haunts you like the man in the hallway haunted me? What thoughts control you and cause you to suffer? It could be thoughts about something someone did to you, or you may be distressed about something someone did to someone else. You could be feeling guilt over something you did. Think about the event and your reaction to it. See if you can find a solution and let go of the painful thoughts, resolve the problem and regain peace of mind. If you are puzzled, close your eyes. Go to a dark and silent place, away from the emotions, light a candle and see what healing images you find or what words you hear to solve your puzzle.

ii

A Potent Weapon

Why we should love our enemies

WE NEED TO LEARN TO LOVE OURSELVES so we can love others. But which others? Our families and friends—that's obvious. But does it really matter whether we love people outside our immediate circle? Is there any reason to love our enemies? How about the people who hurt us and our loved ones?

There is just one answer to questions about whom we must love: everyone. We cannot pick and choose. If we want true peace of mind, we must try to love all living beings.

Consider what seems like an extreme case first: people who wrong you or want to hurt you. Jesus said, "Love your enemies." Why did he give us such strange advice? He wasn't just urging us to be noble or righteous. He advised us to love our enemies because he understood that love is the great obliterator. Love is never destructive. It never harms anyone, but it does obliterate and eliminate. When you love your enemies, they don't exist anymore. You haven't ended their lives, but you have eliminated them as enemies. You have killed them with the most potent weapons: kindness and love.

Love is more powerful and much harder to handle than anger. If that seems like an odd statement, try using love next time you are in a difficult situation. Anger is easy to use and people know how to respond to it—usually with more anger. But try using love and see how powerful its effect is on your adversary.

I have seen the effects of love in many difficult situations. Once when a psychotic patient was screaming obscenities at me, I looked him in the eye and said, "I love you." He stopped yelling and returned to his room and closed the door. When angry flight attendants argued with me over the size of our luggage, I said, "I need your love," and they helped me carry our luggage aboard and stow it. When a young man, angry over the heavy traffic, was screaming obscenities at me through my open car window, I said, "I am sorry you have not been loved, but I love you." He ran back to his car and drove away.

I saw a woman with breast cancer learn about the power of love. She'd grown up in an abusive, alcoholic family and felt bitterness toward her parents. She had been a difficult adolescent, and her parents were as angry at her as she was at them. When the young woman developed cancer, she changed her attitude and decided to love her parents in spite of the harm they'd done her. Her mother moved into her home, and every morning as the young woman left for work she would tell her mother she loved her. The mother never answered. One morning, after three months of saying, "I love you," the daughter was late for work and rushed out of the house. Her mother followed her to the door and yelled out to her, "You forgot something." "What did I forget?" the woman asked. "You forgot to say I love you." She returned, they cried, embraced and healed.

There are cases where a child has been murdered and the victim's parents forgave the murderer and went to visit him in jail. In some cases the murderer accepted the forgiveness and repented. In other cases the murderers were so distressed by being forgiven and loved that they refused to accept the family's visits. In all cases the family that forgave and went on loving rid itself of an enemy and was able to heal and live fulfilling lives in spite of their loss. Now the criminal had the problem, being a victim of love, probably something he had never experienced before and did not know how to handle.

Love has a warming effect on even the coldest of hearts. Hatred never does anyone any good. It is bad for the hated and worse for the hater. Love is good for both the lover and the loved. Use love in good health and remember, when you find yourself confronting enemies, to do what Norman Vincent Peale did. When he died in his nineties, someone said about him, "He outlived his enemies." The response was, "No, he outloved them."

If you want to pack a one-two punch and be undefeatable, add the power of laughter to the power of love. No one can stand up to those two for long. I could go on telling stories of people who were saved from assaults and robberies by forgiving and loving. Even if it doesn't work, does it feel better to die hating or loving?

iii
Does It Matter Who Loves You?

Love your neighbor, your family and the unlovable

LOVE HEALS. LOVE GIVES MEANING TO LIFE. Love is vital to our survival. Love has all these wonderful benefits, which is not surprising when you think about the love between a parent and a child or between two lifelong spouses. But the remarkable thing about love is how little it matters who does the loving. Love does not have to come from a devoted parent or an adoring spouse to be life-enhancing. I hear many stories from people who are alive and thriving today because someone loved them, and that important someone was a schoolteacher, a doctor, a grandparent, a friend, a therapist—the list goes on and on. There are many relationships in which you can provide or receive the love that heals and builds self-esteem and makes life meaningful. The miracle is not love at first sight, but love for a lifetime despite our imperfections.

As a physician, I have had many patients who were self-destructive. No matter how difficult they were I asked them to come see me again and I continued to work with and care for them even when it appeared obvious they didn't care about themselves. Many began to take better care of themselves when they realized they were important to someone—even though that someone was only their doctor. In the work I do now, an answered letter or a returned phone call may save a life because it says, "I care about you." The response is what counts, not the advice.

How much can love accomplish? Can a single parent raise a child? Can gay parents raise a child? Can an abused, suicidal child recover? The answer to each of those questions is "Yes, with love." Blood relationships, gender or ethnic background, terrible experiences or even physical abuse—none of these things matter as much as the question of whether the child has someone to love her. If there is someone to love the child, there is hope for her growing up with self-love and self-esteem and the ability to love others.

Remember that difficult people need your love as much as people who are easy to love. My classic example is a patient of mine who was always bitter and resentful about everything. In the hopes she would gain some perspective, I suggested that she go through the housing project for the elderly she lived in and find someone who was worse off than she was. "Watch what happens to you when you help someone else," I said.

She toured the project, came back to the office and said, "I went through the whole project and there's nobody sicker, with more troubles than me." I knew then that she was almost certainly not ready to experience the joy of helping others. The thought of being well was threatening to her. She didn't want to give up pain and sickness because that was the way she got people to pay attention to her, and that was the closest she came to being loved.

Difficult children misbehave in part because they want attention. From their perspective, getting attention for misbehaving is better than getting none at all. Our job is to keep loving difficult children and to look for ways to give them attention when they are not being difficult. You hope they'll eventually discover they can count on your love and don't have to misbehave to get your attention.

While you are caring for the difficult child in your family or classroom, don't forget to find time for the cooperative child. It is easy to overlook children who are no trouble, but the easily loved children need your love, too. Even angels need attention and love, now and then. Remember how the prodigal son's brother felt.

Loving your family can sometimes be harder than loving your enemies. With your family, you are likely to become emotional and start to impose on them, because after all you love them and you only want what's best for them. As a loving parent, it is tempting to give lots of advice. "Go to law school. Be a doctor. Get married. Live here. Live there. Do this or do that."

Please, resist the urge to direct your children's lives. Remember that love that imposes is not love. True love is not conditional. You can actually kill your children by imposing a life on them. Very young children may hear in your message a suggestion that your love and care depend on their willingness to live the life you choose for them. They think to themselves: "My parents won't provide for me or care for me, so I'll give up my life to please them and be what they want." Then as adults they may become stuck in a life they've chosen not for themselves but for their parents.

You may remember the song with the line, "Accentuate the

positive and eliminate the negative." That's a description of how to love your family. Instead of criticizing your child's unhealthy behavior and telling her what she shouldn't do, tell her you love her and you wish she would take good care of the daughter you love, because you don't want anything bad to happen to her.

Our son Keith and his wife, Jane, taught me this by the way they are raising their son, Charlie. Keith pointed out the difference between saying, "Don't do that" and "Please be careful and safe." One is critical and the other says, "I love you." I wish I had known the difference as a parent. I'm about ready to raise children now, and I'm a generation late. Another reason to wait until we are sixty to raise children.

To be loving, we must think about our actions as well as our words. I recently saw the school lunch menu printed in the local newspaper and was appalled to see the high-fat, high-calorie selections devoid of fresh fruits and vegetables. I wrote the school board and warned them that twenty years from now they may be sued by the people they are feeding today.

The message those meals send is as bad as the physical effects of fats and sugar and caffeine. When we tell the children, through our actions, "We don't care what you eat," we are also telling them we don't love them. When we offer good meals that say, "We care about your health," then we are sending a message of love.

Think about the last time you criticized someone in your family. Now think about the last time you said or did something to let that same person know you love him or her. Which do you do more often? Think about how you could change your recent criticism to be a loving request that accentuates the positive and eliminates the negative. Before you speak, ask what a loving grandmother would say now.

iv
You Don't Put Your Patients to Sleep

When everything else fails, prescribe love

A NUMBER OF YEARS AGO Oscar, our family dog, was close to death with a malignant melanoma. Our vet said he had never seen a dog that sick recover. I discussed with our children putting Oscar to sleep, but they refused to go along with the plan because, they pointed out, "You don't put your patients to sleep." They suggested that we treat Oscar as one of my patients—that we touch him often, feed him by hand and give him vitamin supplements. I brought Oscar home and of course the children went out to play. Oscar lay there on the floor too weak to stand. I spoon-fed him special meals by hand, shared my vitamins with him, massaged and loved him. Within a week, Oscar recovered enough to rise from his sickbed, go outside and live several more happy years playing in our yard with the children and our other pets. He eventually died of "old age."

Sometimes the care older people get is not as loving as the care we give our pets. That's why veterinarians see more miracles than doctors. A few years ago my father-in-law was dying in a nursing home. He was in his nineties, quadriplegic, suffering severe abdominal pain, and unable to keep food down. Tests did not provide a diagnosis, but I assumed he was dying of an intra-abdominal cancer we couldn't detect. We asked that he not be given any heroic treatments that would increase and prolong his suffering.

We wanted to keep him comfortable in his final days and
spend as much time with him as possible, so when a new nursing home was completed close to our home we decided to
move him. The staff of his old nursing home was opposed, and
insurance regulations made the transfer difficult. I finally gave
up on the insurance and assumed financial responsibility,
thinking he had only a short time left to live and the most
important thing was having him close by.

So we moved him to the new home and the staff there had
time to spend with him and realized right away what a wonderful, courageous man he was. His sense of humor returned.
He developed a wonderful rapport with the staff and received a
lot of attention. Like Oscar, his pain went away, he regained
his appetite and he did beautifully in his new home.

So now I am responsible for the medical care payments. I
asked him why he had been dying at the other nursing home.
My father-in-law said, "They were tired of taking care of me. I
was dying to make life easier for them." He was a sweet man,
but I don't approve of his reason for almost dying before his
time. However, his case is not unusual. For every younger person who commits suicide, there are many older people who
deteriorate and die before they have to because they don't feel
loved and have come to feel like a burden.

My father-in-law was not being treated badly in his first
nursing home, but he felt he was a burden. He had to be changed
and fed several times every day. In the new home, he felt he was
appreciated. After the move my father-in-law lived on happily for
several years until, at the age of ninety-seven, he tired of life and
died peacefully. When love is involved, no one is a burden. If that
weren't true, who would have the patience to care for an infant?

I have worked with many people close to death and have
reassured them, when necessary, that it is okay to go when they

are ready. Sometimes I have urged family members to tell a sick, tired and sore person that the family will be okay and it is all right for him to go. But the opposite message is important, too. When the people we love are aging and ill, we should let them know that we love them and need their love as long as we and they are alive. It is also the only thing that remains after they are gone.

v

God Help Me

Where to look for God's love, guidance and assistance, and what to do with it when you find it

THERE'S AN OLD JOKE ABOUT A DROWNING MAN who calls out for God's help. God hears the man and answers, "Have faith. I'll save you, my son."

The man hears God and is relieved. He stops thrashing, screaming and struggling to stay afloat. "God will save me," he thinks. His panic subsides and he refuses help from everyone who comes by to rescue him, saying, "God will save me." He finally drowns, and when he gets to heaven he asks God, "Why didn't save me like you promised?" And God says, "Dummy, I sent you a raft, a boat and a helicopter."

Another fellow who'd been lost in the Arctic was giving a lecture at an explorers' club. "Before I passed out in the snow, I prayed to God to save me, but He didn't." Someone in the audience said, "But you're alive and you're here." "Yes, I know," the explorer said. "An Eskimo saved me."

Why was he so sure that God didn't save him in Her own way, according to Her own plan? Who are we to decide how God acts and rules? We are not in charge of life and nature.

God is in everyone and everything. When we save each other or guide each other or just love each other, we are doing God's work. So God dresses in Eskimo clothing or other disguises, and responds to us whether or not we are aware enough to hear, see or feel Her loving guidance. Everything is a tool of God, from DNA to the weather.

My mother seemed to know God's plans intimately. Whenever I would come to her with a complaint about how my life was going, she would say, "It was meant to be. God is redirecting you. Something good will come of this."

I spent a lot of time as a youth talking to God about how bad Her plan seemed to my way of thinking. This was in my prefaith era, and I did not want to repeat the Job experience. I did not want to be told that there is a big plan I can't understand and that I should have faith, rejoice in my difficulties and accept God's plan whether or not it made sense to me. When I didn't get into my first-choice college, medical school or internship program, my mother seemed sure this was all God's plan. So I went where my mother and God wanted me to go and it worked out beautifully, thank God. I learned that my intellectual choices were no match for God's wisdom.

Remember the Marine Corps survival guide? Remember the item about the group: Look out for the group before you look out for yourself. This is as important in day-to-day life as in a crisis If you look out primarily for yourself, you may measure success by how much money you make or how many impressive things you accumulate.

A better measure of a successful life is how much you have contributed to your group. When I say "your group" I do not mean your battalion or your family or your fellow citizens. Your group is the human race and creation. I said at the beginning of this chapter that we should love all living things. I personally spend time and money trying to help other species survive, endangered or not, but my primary group is the human race. I help other species because their survival and ours are interrelated.

Work is valuable and meaningful when we do it not for our own sake but to help others survive and live meaningful lives. When you have finished an act, ask yourself, "Was that worth doing?" If the task has some value for the group, you will find yourself answering, "Yes." When you do things to enrich yourself or to impress the neighbors, you will not be able to answer consistently, "Yes, that was worthwhile." What are you here to do and what does life require of you? Ask yourself every day how you may serve so your life will be meaningful.

Studies of volunteers have shown there is a benefit to performing acts of love for other people. The irony is that it is actually in your best interest to be selfless. The things you do for the benefit of others not only make you feel fulfilled, they increase your chances of living a long and happy life. Remember that an act of love always benefits at least two people.

vi
Parent, Family Man, Lover

What words do you want inscribed on your headstone?

WHAT ARE YOUR FAVORITE WORDS? Why did you select them? Are they interesting words you find helpful in Scrabble games, or do they have meanings and feelings associated with them that make them your favorites? If you put them on your headstone, would people passing by know something about your life?

The word "love" is at the top of my list of favorite words. I have learned much about life by trying to be loving. The words "parents" and "family" are also on my list of favorites. The dictionary describes a parent as your biological mother or father. But that is not the whole story. Many biological parents never do any parenting, and some people do a lot of parenting without that genetic link. A young woman once bestowed on me the honor of being her CD, or Chosen Dad. I became her parent and was able to provide her with the unconditional love she felt she never received from her biological parents. I do not judge or blame her parents, because they had parents, too, and I know they had other problems that affected their ability to be loving parents.

My third favorite word, "family," is all-inclusive. The dictionary says "family" refers to people related through blood or marriage, but I say a family is created when you make a commitment to the well-being of another living being. Whether or not it is legally certified as in marriage is not the issue. I see families created every day when we come together to help one another.

The family of man includes all of God's creations. Bobbie left a shopping list on the kitchen counter with an item that said, "Chicken for children." Our children are grown and out on their own, so I asked her what that meant. She said, "I want to get some pieces of chicken for the cats." In our view, family isn't limited to *Homo sapiens*. We just adopted a homeless black rabbit. Bobbie named him Smudge. Every pet we have has a name; they are family. Family includes all the living things God has created. So even if your biological family is gone or rejects or abuses you, you still have a family that loves you. I have seen suicidal children share their pain, find the love of a new family and a new life free of bitterness and resentment. You can, too.

For me a family is a group who loves and accepts you despite your faults. It is a group in which you can test yourself. You can argue, disagree and fight with family, because once you are family you remain part of the family no matter what you do. You may be the part other family members prefer not to talk about. They may shake their heads in disbelief at you, but once you are family you remain family, even if you embarrass them.

Family is what life is about. It provides us immortality. Your participation in your family is not limited by the years you are physically present, because you touch generations to come when you are a parent, family member and lover.

Parent. Family man. Lover. I wouldn't mind having those words on my headstone. They tell more about me than any biographical sketch. I try to be those three words.

What are you trying to embody? Pick out a short list of words for your headstone. My list is nouns—parent, family man, lover—but yours can include adjectives or verbs as well. Just keep it short and to the point about what was most important in your life.

vii

What Kind of a Father Would Do Something Like That?

The foundation to build your love on

THE QUESTION OF WHOM YOU SHOULD LOVE has an unambiguous answer: your enemies, your friends, your family, your cats, the living things that give their lives to nourish you, yourself—your job is to love them all. Okay, what is love, and how do you go about it?

First of all, loving someone is not the same as liking someone. No one ever said we have to like everyone. This is good news, because it is impossible to like everyone. Luckily, we only have to love everyone. This is difficult enough but it is not impossible if you have the right relationship with God.

What is the relationship that brings you peace, love and happiness?

Suppose you are sitting along in your living room when you hear a voice say, "Abe, I need to talk to you."

"Honey, did you say something?" you call to the kitchen.

"No dear, I'm making dinner."

"Abe, it's Me," the voice says. "This is your Lord speaking."

"What is it, God? Is it really you? What do you want?"

"I want you to sacrifice your son Ike to prove your faith and love for me."

The request is a difficult one that contains a lesson only if the voice speaking to you is really the Creator. So assume you know it is God and not a schizophrenic episode. Now what do you say? There are many possible responses. Which would you choose?

You could answer God, "My wife would never agree to it."

Or, "It'll be a pleasure; the kid is a nogoodnik anyway."

Or, "I don't work for you anymore if you ask me to do such a thing."

Or, "I love him too much to do that."

Or, "I will give you my life if you want but not his."

Or, "Isn't there something else I can offer you?"

Or, "Yes, Lord."

You can see Abraham had many options. He had time to think and not act out of fear. So how could he say yes to his

Lord? This is not just a question about the son he loved but about his entire life and its meaning. It raises all the big questions: Who or what is your Lord? Do you trust and believe in your Lord enough to follow His voice when it speaks to you? When you see Rembrandt's painting of a bound Isaac with Abraham standing over him with his raised knife, you can appreciate the profound faith revealed by both Abraham and Isaac. They had faith in their Lord and the final outcome.

The Abraham and Isaac story is about faith. For better or worse, we base our lives on faith. Everything we do is directed by the things we believe in. What are your beliefs? If your faith in God is as strong as Abraham's, you will live a life based on kindness, creativity and love.

How can you have faith in a loving God and still say yes when you are asked to sacrifice your son? That is a hard question, but I think Abraham and Isaac both knew they were being tested and that it was very unlikely, though possible, God would have asked them to follow through with the sacrifice. They were prepared to go ahead if necessary because they trusted that their Lord had the greater good in mind, and therefore any act He asked them to perform would serve a beneficial purpose.

If you place your faith in the wrong lord—if you serve money, fear or power, for instance—you will do many destructive things. But when you say yes to the right lord an angel will appear (as one did for Abraham) to show you that destructive acts are not necessary. When you demonstrate your faith, and act out of love, your actions will be good for us all.

Why do I believe Abraham and Isaac both had a pretty good idea what the result of their trip up the mountain would be? If Isaac didn't know what was happening, he might have grown suspicious at the absence of a sacrificial lamb. I think he knew. He was not a helpless child and he did not have to willingly follow his father. He could have left. As for Abraham, if he thought he was going to have to follow through with the sacrifice, he would not have said to his helpers, "We will return." If he was going to kill his son, a more likely statement would have been, "I'll be back shortly."

Abraham and Isaac went to the mountain with complete faith in their Lord. If you find the true Lord and trust Him and put your faith in Him, you will live a life filled with hope, peace and love. You will receive the care and protection of God in return for your display of faith, and you may create a unified family of man.

Read the story of Abraham and Isaac in Genesis 22. Think about their faith and the Lord they trusted. Ask yourself, What do I believe in? Who is my Lord? Do you believe enough and trust enough to listen when your Lord speaks to you?

I now realize that you are a vehicle. A vehicle can take you places, but it needs energy to get started. Faith is the battery cable that connects you to your energy source, God. Faith is needed to start you up and keep you running. Remember your new parable, and remain connected by battery cables to the only battery that never needs recharging.

viii
Death of a Two-Year-Old

What love isn't

LOVE IS NEVER DESTRUCTIVE, but we sometimes do destructive things and claim we are acting in the name of love. The danger comes when we confuse love with emotionalism. Yes, love is connected to feelings, but it is not simply about your passions or emotions.

Love is a concern for the well-being of the loved one. Love is giving with no expectations. Love is doing what God requires and not just being good or acting properly. Love cures, heals and rewards two people: the lover and the beloved. Emotionalism carries no such guarantees.

Our daughter, Carolyn, saved an injured pigeon's life. She named it George and kept it in our house and nursed it until it was well again and able to fly. The day it flew away, she was saddened but full of joy. That's love. If you save someone's life and then check the mailbox every day or wait for the telephone to ring because you are expecting a thank-you—that's not true love. That's self-interest. Love is its own reward. You can feel and see its benefits.

It is easy to think you are being loving when you are really looking out for your own interests. For many years I have been trying to be as loving a person as I can be, but it wasn't until a two-year-old named Missy came to live with us that I learned that my need to be loving can cause problems.

Missy had been living at our son's house, where some construction was creating noise and commotion. Missy was frightened and spent her days hiding from the workmen. I thought she would do better at our house, but Bobbie and Jeff didn't think moving her was a good idea. I was sure we could offer her a better home during the construction, so I kept bringing the idea up until first Jeff agreed and then finally Bobbie relented.

So we brought Missy to our house where she was among other like-minded youngsters. She still seemed upset and frightened, but I assured Bobbie that Missy was just getting used to a strange environment and that she'd settle in and be happier than she'd been at Jeff's house. At first my plan seemed to be working. Missy came out of hiding, and although she kept to herself she didn't look uncomfortable. True, she had lost her appetite and ate very little, but she was overweight and I figured it wouldn't hurt her to lose a few pounds.

We gave Missy a few more days to settle in. She continued to avoid the other youngsters, but I insisted that was part of her adjustment period. Eventually, Bobbie realized that Missy was having more than an adjustment problem. "She's sick," Bobbie said. So we took Missy to her doctor and sure enough she was jaundiced. He asked why I hadn't noticed. I said, "Because Missy is not the same skin color we are."

The doctor hospitalized Missy and she went through a difficult time, ultimately dying of liver failure. I have to tell you now that Missy was a cat. We've had cats and other animals around the house for years, so I'd faced the loss of a pet before. But Missy's death really tore my heart out because I knew my emotionalism was the reason for her death. I'd brought her to our house, ignored the advice of others and missed her symptoms because I wanted so badly to be able to care for her. My need to display what I thought was love was fatal for Missy. Had I sought help sooner, her nutritional balance could have been restored and her liver damage reversed.

This was a painful, powerful experience for me. I still have Missy's collar and tag on my desk to remind me what I learned. Sometimes you have to stop and think about whether you are really acting out of love for another. You have to analyze your feelings and look at the results of your actions. Remember that true love never injures or destroys living things. Are your actions truly loving? When emotions guide your judgment and decision-making, you are not thinking of the well-being of others. Then you are dangerous. When love guides your actions, you won't cause the kind of trouble I caused Missy. Are you devoted to what you want or the needs of another?

ix
Faith and Fear

More of what love isn't

FEAR AND LOVE DO NOT MIX. If you are guided by fear, you are very likely going to do harmful things to the people you fear, yourself and others. Some fearful people are so destructive they kill needlessly out of a misplaced impulse to protect themselves. You can't trust fearful people—this is true in the Mafia, the Marines, gangs, jobs and concentration camps. Survivors do not act out of fear. They act out of faith. In whom or what do you place your faith so you do not have to live in fear?

Two parables I first heard on Clarissa Pinkola Estes tapes illustrate the way love can help you overcome fear. In one, the only thing that can heal a sick man is milk from a lioness. In the other, a man comes home from the war with post-traumatic stress disorder and his wife doesn't know how to help him. A healer tells her to make a potion that contains a hair plucked from the chest of a bear. In both stories, the heroes overcome their fear and bring back their prize. Motivated by love, they find the inner strength, faith, patience and calmness to help heal a loved one.

In the first parable, the lioness recognizes the hero's strength and yields without a struggle. Her milk heals the sick man, just as promised. In the second story, the wife spends months feeding the bear, sitting nearer and nearer the cave, until she finally gets close enough to pluck a hair. When she takes her prize to the healer, the healer promptly throws it in the fire. The wife asks, "Why was I sent out to risk my life for something that you immediately discarded?" The teacher in that parable tells the wife, "What you need to do now is be as caring, patient, calm and loving with your husband as you were with the bear."

Have faith and do not fear. I am not suggesting that you run out to pluck a hair from a bear's chest. But I will tell you that when you put your fears aside you are able to love more fully, and when you love enough you will find you have nothing to fear.

While I never want fear to dominate my life, I will say one good thing about it: Fear, at times, can be a great motivator. Our natural fears protect us from dangerous heights and loud sounds. It is amazing how fast a tired jogger can run when a dog gives chase. I know from experience that fatigue disappears and strength is restored when the dog appears.

In a little booklet about handling tough times, Norman Vincent Peale tells the story of a man who worked the second shift and fearlessly walked home through a cemetery every night. One night he fell into a newly dug grave and couldn't climb out because of loose soil. Being fearless, he put his coat around his shoulders and sat down calmly to wait for the gravediggers to arrive in the morning. A short while later, another man fell into the far end of the open grave and began trying to jump and climb out. The first man listened to the second man's futile efforts, and then said, "Boy, you'll never get out that way." At the sound of a voice in the darkness, the terrified second man leaped out of the grave and ran away.

I agree with Norman that fear can be a powerful motivator, but to live constantly in fear is to live a slow death. It is far better to live in faith. Faith can protect you from menacing dogs and can help you climb out of any hole, and faith has no destructive side effects.

Faith helps you survive by giving you a companion: God. It gives you the belief in yourself also—that you have the inner strength to survive attacks. It frees you to go out into the troubled world knowing you will not be a victim. To have faith in yourself frees you to live your life.

Faith empowers, encourages and leads to transcendence, ecstasy and freedom from pain even when you are attacked. Look at the martyrs who had faith and went through tortures much worse than a dog bite. They faced death bravely because they had faith. As the rabbis say, "When the choice is between wisdom and faith, choose faith." Wisdom is a good thing but it has its limits. Faith has no limits, and its power transcends the problems of daily life.

What are you afraid of? Illness? Loss of a job? The death of a loved one? Changes in your family? Aging? Your children leaving home? Blindness? Decide what you fear most. Then look around you. Whatever you fear, it has already happened to other people and some of them are living successfully with it. Find them. Volunteer at a nursing home or work with the handicapped. Find people who are living successfully with whatever it is you fear, and let these people be your teachers.

x
Devotion

What love is

WHAT ARE YOU DEVOTED TO? The answer determines what kind of life you will have and how much joy you will find.

When I devote myself to changing other people, I have endless problems. I am compelled to correct them. I feel I have to criticize them when they aren't helpful and loving enough, or when they aren't spiritual enough or don't clean up after themselves. Improving the world by trying to improve other people is hard work that leaves me feeling lousy. In the end, no one, not even me, lives up to my expectations.

Loving means devoting yourself to people, but not to changing them. When I devote myself to the people in my life all our lives improve. While I am telling them how to meet my expectations, no one is happy. As soon as I accept them as they are and start caring about them and trying to make their lives easier, everyone is happier and wonderful things start happening.

Joseph Campbell told a story about overhearing a man in a restaurant telling his child how to eat. "Why don't you let him do what he wants to do?" the man's wife asked.

"Because I've never done anything I wanted to do in my life," the man answered.

Campbell contrasted that story with a passage in Sinclair Lewis's novel *Babbitt*. In Lewis's story, a young man decides not to go to college. He wants to get married and get a factory job because he likes working with his hands. His family is giving him a hard time about his decision, but his father takes him aside and tells him he has never done anything he wanted to do in his life. Now, even though the father isn't happy with the son's choices, he tells him he admires his decision to live his life the way he wants to live it. Then he puts his arm around his son and they go back into the room to face the family. I gave a copy of that passage to every one of our five children.

The more children you have, the harder it is to direct everyone's actions. With five children, you are too busy to tell everyone what to do and it is easier just to watch them grow and blossom.

Our oldest son once asked why I treated the younger children differently than I'd treated him at their age: "How come
they don't have to do what I had to do?"

"Because I've learned that a lot of the things I asked you to
do aren't important." Then I apologized for my inexperience as
a father. He accepted my apology because my newfound wisdom made his life easier, too.

Today I am amazed at the things our children have done
and their wide range of interests. They are all living their lives
and not the ones I would have planned for them. But I have
learned their lives are theirs, not mine, and in living their own
lives they have given me experiences and an education I would
never have had if I'd been fool enough to make them do what I
thought they should do.

*What are you devoted to? Think about someone in your fam-
ily whom you love. How do you behave toward this person?
Think about your interactions over the past few days. Are you
trying to change her and improve her? Or are you watching
her grow and enjoying her and trying to make her life easier?*

xi

Deafness Is Darker by Far

More on what love is and what it does

MY MOTHER IS LOSING HER SIGHT and can no longer see dirt on
her kitchen floor. That is a benefit in my mother's case because
it allows her to relax and not worry about every speck of dust.

Love has the same beneficial blinding effect. It allows us to relax and blinds us to the flaws and scars in everyone. When we decide to love, we can step back and stop judging everyone and appreciate their beauty instead. Lovers are like parents to the world, or perhaps I should say grandparents, since grandparents are less likely to be judgmental. What the world needs is a corps of loving grandparents to restore everyone's self-esteem.

One morning my wife pointed out six or seven cups whose handles had broken off because of how I'd loaded them into the dishwasher. I sometimes still act like a compulsive surgeon, and I showed her how you could still drink from them, without handles. I could tell we were headed for marriage counseling again if I didn't get them out of her sight, so I hid the broken cups and later stored them away in a cupboard in our vacation house. The next time we went on vacation I went jogging early in the morning so I wouldn't be there when Bobbie discovered the cups. On my run I saw a cup with a broken handle lying in the road. I knew God had placed it there for me, because in twenty-five years of jogging on this road, I had never found a cup. I ran over, picked it up and saw that the cup featured a picture of two chubby elephants hugging each other. The caption below read: "I love you just the way you are."

The cups with the broken handles are still in our vacation house because Bobbie's eyesight suddenly deteriorated when I brought home the broken elephant cup. She can still see as well as ever, but she is blind to the flaws in the cups and in me, thank goodness.

I don't prescribe anything for a person afflicted with love blindness. I just tell them it can be highly contagious, so they should expose their family and start an epidemic.

My mother is also losing her hearing, and she, like Helen Keller, finds deafness is darker by far than blindness. Mom goes a step further and says she feels stupid when she can't hear what people are saying and can't respond appropriately.

I can think of nothing good about deafness, either in a physical or a metaphorical sense. Deafness is especially destructive when it is caused by a refusal to listen to others or promptly forgetting everything that is said. Don't think that type of deafness goes unnoticed. People close to you know when you are listening and whether you are hearing what they are saying. If your family wants to be united and at peace with one another, you must all work hard at listening to one another.

In a family that is united, physical deafness is not an insurmountable obstacle. You can hear your loved ones no matter how poorly your ears work. I know deaf people who are able to hear with their hearts. And I know people with perfect ears who drive their families crazy with their lack of hearing. I know about this firsthand because our children used to get upset when I read the paper and watched television while they were talking to me. They'd say, "Dad, you're not listening." I would repeat all the things they said to prove I was listening, but they told me that being able to repeat their words was not the same thing as *hearing* them. Hearing means listening attentively to what they had to say.

Today when one of the children wants to talk to me, I put down the paper, turn off the television and listen to what he has to tell me. The children have learned that when I have things I need to do my hearing deteriorates if their monologue goes on too long.

I also have learned how to say "m-m-m" in many ways and to stop trying to solve everyone's problems. They thank me for listening. It helps them to clarify and solve their problems.

Practice saying "m-m-m" in many ways. It will help your family and bring you praise for the wisdom they discover.

xii

It's Light and Takes Up No Space

The one thing you can take with you

WHAT WILL WE TAKE WITH US on the ultimate journey? It's fairly obvious that we cannot take material things with us wherever we go. Just as airlines restrict your luggage and the trunk of your car has a limited capacity, so, too, heaven has space problems. Love is the only thing I know of that has an unlimited capacity, is weightless and takes up no space.

I believe love does go with us wherever we go. It is the one thing that is immortal and not limited by the physical body's existence. When I say it goes where we go, I mean when our body no longer exists our love continues on. Our love goes with us wherever our spirit, soul and thoughts go, but it also stays in the lives of those we have touched. Love is energy and is not limited by the laws that apply to material things or associated with time. Thus you can take it with you and at the same time leave it behind. Love is the bridge between the land of the living and the land of the dead.

Best of all, perhaps, the love we leave behind remains strong and can grow long after we are gone. In a study of Harvard students, researchers found that of the students who described their parents as loving, only twenty-nine percent suffered a significant illness in the thirty-five years after leaving school. Of the students who did not feel loved by their parents, a remarkable ninety-eight percent had experienced a significant illness in the same thirty-five years. This study took into account other variables such as smoking, divorce, death of a parent and so on.

We can give love and receive it, take it with us or leave it behind. Love cultivates and sustains lives and exerts its effect long after we are gone. Love is like the light that shines from a torch we hold aloft. It shines on what lies ahead, what is at our side and what we have left behind. The illuminating power of love doesn't defy the laws of physics—it made them.

What do you want to take with you on the ultimate journey? What do you really need to bring along, once your body no longer exists? We've all heard the saying, "You can't take it with you." But assume for a minute you can take it with you— anything you want, material or intangible. Can you think of anything you would rather have than the love you have given and received? If you can think of something better, write me a note and tell me what it is.

xiii
Who Is Your Family and Where Is Your Home?

What does love have to do with it?

HAVE YOU EVER WONDERED why God created one man and one woman at the beginning of creation? We are told there were many animals and plants in the beginning, so what's the point of starting with only one man and one woman?

I think the creation story is pointing out that we are all one family. This news upsets some people, but it is the truth. We are all branches of the same family tree, have the same roots, even if our fruits, leaves and blossoms vary.

Just as there is a variety of trees with a variety of branches and leaves and fruits and nuts, so our family tree has branched out and diversified. Every family tree bears its share of fruits and nuts. But despite our diversity we all remain the same inside. You can't tell from a photograph of someone's insides what race, religion, sex or nationality he is. I think we should hang a photograph of a chest cavity in public buildings along with the portraits of famous men and women. This would remind us of our common origins and our basic similarities.

I like being part of the family of humans, but I am sometimes discouraged by the way our family behaves. We show so little respect for our planet and its other life forms. As I travel I see litter and garbage that has been tossed out of cars. What are people thinking? Why don't they care about life? Even if they don't respect or care about themselves, why do people destroy the environment and spoil things for generations not yet born? My sense is that the people in our family who litter and pollute the environment are resentful and are being destructive as a sneaky way of getting even for the love and compassion they never received.

I don't know how to awaken people and get them to think about how their behavior affects the rest of the family and the other living things who share our family home. I don't think threats and punishments do much good. Maybe instead of signs that say, "No Littering, $500 Fine," we should put signs along the roadside saying, "We Love You," "God Loves You," and "What Do You Want to Be Remembered For?"

Many of us have pleasant memories of growing up in a family: sharing a bathroom or bedroom with siblings, eating together, shoveling snow, using up the hot water, cluttering up the house with toys, living with pets, being disturbed by the noise of family and neighbors, cleaning the house. Bobbie and I have five children, so we have lots of family memories. What would happen if we stopped to think about our favorite home-and-family memories, and then tried to look at the planet as our home and all humans as our family?

Our family includes our descendants—our future grand-children and great-grandchildren and nieces and nephews, and every other human and nonhuman being who will ever live on this planet. If we remember that our family extends into the future, maybe we will do a better job of taking care of the family dwelling we will be leaving to our children.

5
Thriving in Bad Times

i
That's Good

Why we should be thankful for our problems

THE CEO OF A LARGE COMPANY had an excellent financial adviser who had one strange habit. After the adviser gave his advice, he always told the CEO that whatever happened was good. No matter what happened to the company's sales or profits or stock, no matter what reports came in from field offices, no matter what campaigns the competitors launched or what lawsuits people brought against the company, the adviser always told the CEO, "That's good."

One day the CEO lost several fingers in an accident. The adviser came to visit him in the hospital, looked at the CEO's bandaged hand and said, "You'll see it's a good thing."

"That's it. Enough is enough," the CEO said. "You're fired. Get out of here."

The CEO returned to work, still upset about the loss of his fingers. When the wound healed he decided to take a break and give himself a gift. He loved to study primitive cultures, so he decided to go on a safari. He hired a guide and porters and with some of his associates set off for the wilds. The first day out, the inexperienced guide lost his way and the group was captured by cannibals. The fires were lit and water put on to boil as the captives were lined up for the ceremonial meal. When the cannibal chief sat down to observe the procedure, he looked at the CEO, saw his missing fingers and stopped the proceedings. "This man is imperfect. We don't eat imperfect people. It would affect our future generations. Release him."

When the CEO returned home he looked up his former adviser and went to see him. He found him unemployed and living off his savings in a house he had rented.

"I came to apologize to you," said the CEO. "You were right."

"What do you mean?" said the adviser.

The CEO told him about the safari and the cannibals and why he was spared. "It really was a good thing that I lost my fingers. I'm so sorry I fired you and ruined your reputation and life. What can I do to make up for my mistake?"

"No, no, it was a good thing you fired me."

"What do you mean it was a good thing I fired you?"

"If you hadn't fired me, I would have gone with you and been eaten by the cannibals."

Someone handed me that story at a seminar. I like it because it makes the same point my mother brought me up on: Good things can come out of adversity. To quote my mom again, "It was meant to be. God is redirecting you. Something good will come of this." A woman in one of our groups was making the same point when she told us about the side effects of cancer. Early in her treatment, this woman wanted to quit chemotherapy because it was making her feel horrible. Her doctor had grumbled, "Well, you know you could die, because cancer has side effects, too."

She told us, "I went home and learned about cancer's side effects, and found that some of them are wonderful." The side effects of her cancer were the faith she rediscovered, the work she did on herself and the relationships she repaired after cancer gave her a wake-up call.

Another man said, "Thank God I have cancer. I could have dropped dead from a heart attack and would have died without learning about love and kindness."

Bobbie and I have several cats living with us, or perhaps I should say that several cats allow us to live with them. In either case, before they were neutered, they would go into heat and meow loudly without pause, rolling around the floor and in general becoming noisy impediments to household activities for several days. I realize that having cats in heat is a small problem compared with having cancer, but the cats were disruptive enough to remind me of one of life's great lessons: Something else can always go wrong, and always will, I can assure you.

At workshops I never found anyone willing to switch problems with any other person. So be thankful for the problems you have, be thankful that you don't have more than you have and don't ever think you're nearing the end of your problems. Remember that your cat can still go into heat. That's the nature of life. Rejoice in it.

I do not want you to sit around trying to imagine what will go wrong next, and how it will benefit you. Life will take care of that for you. I am going to suggest an exercise to help you discover the value of a problem life has already given you. Think about something you wanted in the past that you did not get. Pick something far enough in the past that you can have some perspective about how it turned out and where it led you. Have you ever stopped to think of the benefits it brought, or the things it taught you? Think of things you were directed to do or learn that you wouldn't want to give up. I guarantee that, unless you prefer suffering, you will find very few problems in your past that didn't enrich your life in ways you could not have anticipated at the time. The key is to remain open to the universe's schedule and not get stuck in your own.

ii

Dying Isn't the Worst Outcome

How to survive living or dying

ONE OF OUR CANCER THERAPY GROUPS was discussing life, death and all the problems we have in between. Everyone in the room had problems, and as we talked about them one after another, we all worried about how they would turn out. It was getting depressing until finally one member said, "Dying isn't the worst outcome." Our laughter didn't make our problems go away but it ended our complaining.

On another occasion the same group was pondering their fears and the difficulties of the process of dying when one group member said, "I can survive dying." Again, the laughter healed us.

Another day when fear was overwhelming the group, I asked our oldest member what she feared. The woman, who is in her nineties, sat quietly for a while and then said, "Oh, I know! Driving on the parkway at night." She had already lived through what the rest of us feared—illness, aging, loss of loved ones and increasing frailty—and the only thing she feared was driving at night. Her example gave us the strength to go on. My fear used to be seeing a big dog sitting in the road when I was out jogging. After I was bitten, I discovered that all my fears are worse than the dog's bite.

If living is difficult, dying will be, too. If you live a life of love, service, faith and peace, your death will be a peaceful one. If your life is filled with regret, desire, fear and anger, your death will be difficult. Some people have a difficult time dying because they feel they have failed their family and don't have their permission to die. If you have lived a full life, are tired of your body and want to leave, you don't need anyone's permission. But if you lived a life others chose for you, you'll need their permission to die.

Those who have lived authentic lives, defined by their choices, desires and uniqueness, have a different experience with death. They are full of life to their last moment and die without any difficulties, surrounded by loved ones. Those are good deaths. I do not mean to disregard the grief a family feels. Death is a loss to the living. But some people live so successfully that when it is time to die they simply exercise their freedom to leave a body that is too tired for them to love with. For them, death is the time to turn the set off. Leaving their body is their next treatment. It is a spiritual therapy.

My ninety-seven-year-old quadriplegic father-in-law's death is a good example of what I call "falling up." He lived until he was through with life, refused his dinner and vitamins and died so peacefully and contentedly that evening that, to put it in his words, he just "fell up."

I have seen a critically ill woman wait for her children to fly across the country and reach her side before she died. I have seen a child who was suffering from an incurable cancer wait for her mother's birthday to die as a gift to her mother. "To free you from all the troubles," she said. The mother understood the daughter's need to set herself free, and the gift that her dying represented.

A person falling up is an emotional sight, full of joy and sadness. Have you ever seen a child with a helium balloon let the string slip through his fingers? A sadness is felt over the loss, but the flight into the heavens leaves you with a feeling of grace and wonder. Where is it going? If the balloon is lost indoors it rises to the ceiling and remains trapped. That leaves you with a very different feeling—more frustration than wonder. When the spirit, like the balloon, is free of the gravity of life and mortal love, it rises toward a new relationship, attracted by a greater force than you or I can imagine—the primal lover and final healing. We can only watch with wonder at the spirit's final destination. No ceilings of this world will block its graceful ascent.

iii

I Don't Want to Prune That Tree

Sometimes you have to give up a part of yourself

I HAVE ALWAYS FOUND IT HARD to prune a tree and relatively easy to operate on someone. That may seem coldhearted, but when I am operating on someone I am removing a disease or correcting some defect in the person's body. I can remove dead limbs from trees, but any other pruning is upsetting because I don't want to saw through something that is alive and appears healthy.

One day I was standing in our yard next to our mimosa tree with Jeff, who is a master gardener. "Dad, you need to prune this," Jeff said, pointing to the tree.

The branch he was pointing to was very large and covered with many beautiful blossoms. I told him I didn't mind that it grew at an odd angle. I didn't care about the shape or symmetry of the tree. The branch was alive and bearing blossoms and I didn't want to lose it.

Jeff listened to my impassioned plea and then said, "Dad, if you don't prune the tree, it will die."

Now he was speaking my language. If we were dealing with a threat to the life of my patient, then I could understand my consultant's advice and the need to operate. I got my saw out and removed the limb.

What did Jeff and the mimosa tree teach me about life? There are times when you must be willing to give up a part of yourself to save your life. In some cases, it means literally giving up part of your body or the loss of the use of limbs or organs.

How much you regret giving part of yourself up depends on how you define yourself. It is easier to lose parts of your body if you understand your essence and realize you are more than the sum of your parts. You have a spirit and a soul that cannot be altered by pruning. Yes, the envelope can be altered and the container can be crushed, but the essence remains unaltered. Your faith and love can continue to exist no matter how badly your physical body is damaged.

This is a difficult lesson for most of us. Take a look around and you'll see the people who have gone on living and loving despite disfigurement, paralysis or loss of a limb. If you see their example, learn from them and realize you are a spirit. Then you will understand how to give up physical parts of yourself and still be capable of performing acts for the greater good.

I removed a portion of the lovely mimosa so it could go on providing us with beauty for many years to come. I believe the tree understood this more easily than we do. Whether you are pruned by surgery, aging or disease, accept the fact that you must give up portions of yourself, at times, in order to survive and continue growing toward the light. Remember that losing one part may lead to the enhancement of others. Your work of art is not finished until the day you die.

> *Which part of yourself do you define as you? Are you still your-self after a shaved head? Would you still be yourself if you lost your teeth? A breast? An arm or leg? Your bladder or rectum? What if you had a heart transplant? No matter what physical part you lose, you are still yourself—you are changed, but you are still you. If you feel that pruning any physical part of your-self would mean you are no longer you, then you need to spend some time getting to know your un-prunable essence. Anyone who has had a near-death experience will tell you, you are not your body. Who are you? It is time you found out.*

iv

Do the Wrong Thing First

Mistakes can work for you

MISDIRECTIONS CAN BE A BLESSING, TOO. If you start off by going the wrong way and meet someone you have been looking for, you end up happy about your mistake.

A contractor I know was hired to pave a driveway in a neigh-borhood where he'd never worked before. He paved the drive and then knocked on the door to ask for payment. A woman he'd never seen before came to the door, and after a few moments of confusion the contractor realized he had paved the wrong driveway. The woman said her driveway had needed paving and offered to pay him something, but the contractor refused any payment. He told her he had misread the mailbox, it was his error and that was that. He moved his equipment next door and went to work on the correct driveway.

What do you think the neighbors thought when they heard about the contractor who paved the wrong driveway and refused any payment? Did they think he was inept? That they wouldn't want someone who couldn't find the right address working for them? No, the neighbors all talked about how nice he was and everyone in the neighborhood who needed their driveway paved hired him. He had more business because of his mistake and kindness than from advertising.

Don't let your mistakes discourage you. A mistake is an opportunity to show you have heart. Be willing to say you are sorry. If you follow up your mistakes by doing the right thing, without making excuses, you show everyone you care about them and are responsible and trustworthy.

Think about the mistakes you have made recently. What is the biggest mistake you have made in the past month? What did you do when you realized what you'd done? Did you try to hide it or deny that it was a mistake? Did you make excuses for yourself and blame others? Or did you apologize and set about trying to do the right thing? Think of the most recent mistake you've made, large or small. Have you followed that one up by doing the right thing? If you haven't, it is probably not too late to say, "I'm sorry." The people I continue to work with are those who can acknowledge their faults.

v

Dwelling in the Darkness

The value of pain

WE OFTEN REFER TO THE DIFFICULT TIMES in our lives as dark times. When you lose someone you love or your health deteriorates, when you are abandoned or rejected, or when innumerable difficulties pile up and you sink into depression and hopelessness—in these dark times you may feel you are drowning or being buried alive. Some hours are so dark that you may barely see a faint light at the end of the tunnel, and it may seem almost futile to keep struggling toward it.

Despite the difficulty, the darkest times of our lives are often the most meaningful. These are the times when we cannot deny our fears and we are forced to pay attention to what we are feeling inside. What happens then, when you listen to your feelings and not your intellect? Your problems become your teacher, healer and enlightener. The compost becomes fertilizer.

When you are not afraid to dwell in the darkness, you create fertile ground for change. It is no different from a gardener preparing the ground for planting. But it takes courage to face emotional pain and uncertainty. And it takes wisdom to know that a greater good will come from your willingness to explore what your mind tells you to fear and avoid.

It is tempting to numb the pain or distract ourselves so we won't have to dwell in the darkness and learn from it. If you give into the temptation to use anesthesia, you lose the guidance your feelings can offer. We need our pain to protect and direct us.

Self-analysis may seem at first like surgery without anesthesia, and of course no one wants that experience. Our culture teaches us how to numb and distract ourselves but not how to listen to our pain and learn from our difficulties. Think what we learn about pain from television. We learn that pain is to be avoided at all costs and that there are a variety of pain relievers for every conceivable pain. I would like to see a television commercial that says, "Your pain is a great teacher. Learn from it and be healed."

Do not be afraid to work in your garden. Let your innate intelligence direct you out from under the compost heaped upon you. Your tears will provide the water that softens the soil and leads you to the light. You will then grow straight, tall and free of scars. Now is the right season for growth; be inspired and start toward the light. It is not as far away as it seems. Remember that a seed sees no light, but knows the right direction to grow in. That knowledge and wisdom is in you, too.

Pain that is buried continues to hurt. Physicians, firefighters and nurses all suffer when they bury the pain of their professions deep inside them. Buried pain needs release. I would give the same advice to a war veteran or emergency room physician or police officer or anyone who is storing painful memories: Start to talk and write about the painful event and take the lid off your feelings. Only then can you begin to heal. If you do not, the buried pain will take its toll. You will become a mummy wrapped in pain, blind to life. When the pain is released it makes room for love to come in.

At seminars I sometimes ask people if they'd like total freedom from pain. I warn them, though, that while it may seem like a lovely idea at first, freedom from all emotional and physical pain can be a threat to one's well-being. Stop and think about it: Without pain, how will you know when you are sick, in need of treatment? How will you know if you've been burned, pinched or injured in any way?

There is an important difference between pain and suffering. Suffering is an emotional response. Pain is a physical response that protects and defines you so you take care of yourself and avoid further injury. When you can't avoid injury, pain compels you to get help or treatment. Why are we afraid of something as useful as pain? What makes it unbearable?

The intensity of your pain is related to how you feel about it. Pain is unbearable only when it has no meaning. Listen to your body and learn from it. Talk to your pain, define it and ask what it can teach you. Your pain will always have an answer if you are willing to hear it. When there is conflict in your life and no meaning to the pain, it is very hard to control. I see this in people with problems ranging from headaches to life-threatening diseases. When the discomfort leads them to make the proper life decisions, whether the choice is to live or to die, the pain leaves. It has done its work.

vi
The Source of the Soul's Water

The value of sorrow, grief and suffering

JUST AS YOU CANNOT ESCAPE LIFE'S PROBLEMS, you cannot avoid painful feelings and emotions. What can you do with sorrow and grief? You can accept them into your life the way water is accepted into the ground and taken up by the tree. Let these emotions become a part of your life without asking why. Accept life and death, experience the rituals of grief and sorrow, and free yourself to live. Grief and sorrow bring forth the tears that are the water the soul needs to survive. If you feel no sorrow and no grief, you will dry up and wither away as the tree does in a time of drought.

Survival is not simply about eliminating suffering, but understanding and learning from it. Just as our problems can enrich our lives and our pains teach us, our wounds give us power. They enable us to do things we could not do if we were unscathed by life. Wounds that are still painful lead us to the divine and give us the power to heal and be healers.

We need to accept our wounds and suffering the way a loving mother accepts new life. Embrace your suffering as you would a crying infant. It may break you apart but then you can be reconstructed. If you refuse to suffer or bend, life will kill you. If you suffer, bend or break like a bone, you can heal and develop greater strength at the broken place.

Pain and suffering will pull and push you along your path but they will never leave you directionless. Compassion is your compass. The path of your life cannot be followed with only your intellect as your guide. When darkness surrounds you and you do not know where you are going, remember to close your eyes; only then will you know if you are taking the right path.

vii

Soul Food

The value of illness, depression and misfortune

WHY DO WE DEVELOP CERTAIN SYMPTOMS and illnesses at specific times in our lives? The question has several answers. We can get sick when we are exposed to toxins and pathogens. That answer focuses on external mechanical events, which are certainly part of the picture. But why is one person susceptible when another is not? If we view disease as entirely a chance occurrence or mechanical event, we lose the opportunity to learn from the message of the disease, promote healing and prevent future illnesses.

I am not suggesting that you are to blame for being sick. Guilt, blame and shame are never the appropriate response. I am suggesting that you learn what you can do to get well and stay well. If I have symptoms of laryngitis, as I have had, the message may be that it is time for me to shut down my voice. An injury to my foot might be my body's way of saying, "Slow down." And if I refuse to listen, a dizzy spell is certainly my body's way of telling me, "Lie down before you fall down." If you listen to the message from your body, you recover more quickly and you are less likely to become ill or injure yourself again. The internal environment is a very subtle and awesome field of energy and wisdom about which we still have much to learn. It is a great communicator. I recommend that you listen to your symptoms and follow their directions. Listening takes desire, intention and time. Most of us don't think we have the time to stop to pay attention to our bodies, but I can tell you from experience it is worth the effort.

I am not opposed to standard medications and medical technology. Use all the tools, options and alternatives available to you. Just make sure you include listening to the inner voice of your body—the voice that speaks as a symptom. That voice can testify against your actions, depending on how you live.

Depression is not good for you. It tells your body that living is not desirable, suppresses your immune system and leaves you vulnerable to illnesses and relapses. If you become seriously ill while you are depressed, your chances of recovery are diminished.

Now that I have told you how unhealthy it is to be depressed, the next time you get depressed, will you get even more depressed knowing how bad it is for you? Or will you think about what you can learn from your depression and do what I do: Have a happy depression. You do this by using your depression the same way you use problems, pain and illness: You let it be your teacher. Your depression is trying to push you toward happiness, toward the light at the end of the dark tunnel. It is a form of pressure that can turn charcoal into a diamond. Ask your depression what you are to learn from it, so you will no longer be vulnerable.

When you feel depression coming on, allow yourself to go within and be still. Feel it, learn from it and grow. Tell your family that you are having a happy depression so they will understand why you are quiet and withdrawn. Give it the time it needs to become your teacher and then move on with the insight you have gained.

You can take an antidepressant but that isn't the same as healing yourself. An antidepressant medication may be very helpful and can start you on your healing journey. I am definitely not opposed to its proper use. But the medication may be unnecessary if you try learning from the depression first. If you find you do need medication to correct your body's chemistry, remember that the medicine is only the beginning, and not the entire answer. But there are answers. They already exist within you, and you can find them if you take the time to listen to your feelings. Feelings are not good or bad. They are simply feelings to which we can choose how to respond.

What feeds and nourishes our souls? What teaches us, better than anything else, about the value of life? The answer is not our good fortune, but our misfortune.

I have seen the benefits of misfortune in my own life and the lives of my patients. I have heard patients say their disease is a gift. A recent study of survivors of floods, hurricanes and fires came to the same conclusion. People who saw the calamity as an opportunity to learn about the value of life were better adjusted to the disaster and their losses. The well-adjusted survivors were reminded of their mortality, and they reported that the danger and hardships helped them put their lives in proper perspective. Many who had suffered consider-able losses said their lives were better after the disaster than they had been before.

Our soul and spirit feed on misfortune. If you are willing to learn and grow, you can use disaster to enrich your life. If you persist in focusing on losses and limitations, your soul will not be nourished. On the contrary, it will be starved for spiri-tual food.

I am not suggesting you torture yourself to become enlightened and soulful. Life will provide you all the problems and disasters you need. Misfortunes come in many forms and some come in disguise, masquerading as good fortune. In the next chapter, I'll prepare you for the dangers of good fortune.

Do not go looking for problems to feed your soul. Just let life be your teacher. It will nourish you with its inevitable diffi-culties. How will you know whether you are letting life teach and nourish you? If your physical senses become more sensi-tive to the beauty you see, the words of love you hear, and the life you feel touching your body and soul, then you know you have discovered the great value of misfortune. In the words of Freud, as paraphrased by my wife: "Therapy is to turn neurotic conflicts into normal problems"; Jung: "The point of therapy is to lead a normally disillusioned life"; and Woody Allen: "Life is full of misery, loneliness, unhappiness and suffering and it's all over much too quickly."

viii
Bodies and Minds

Why it makes sense to look for the meaning of an illness

IF YOU THINK OF AN ILLNESS as a purely mechanical process and you doubt that bodies are capable of delivering messages about life, you might be surprised to hear what transplant recipients are reporting. More and more, people who have received new livers, lungs or hearts are starting to reveal that they have uncanny knowledge of the lives of their donors. It sounds incredible at first, but it would seem that organs carry memories of the donor's life.

In one case a child received the heart of a murdered child and then began to have nightmares of the murder scene. Ultimately her new memories and dreams helped identify the person who murdered the donor. In another case a man said jokingly that he must have received an Irish Catholic kidney because after his transplant he knew what the inside of a church across town looked like. He'd never been in the church and his wife thought he was nuts, but he described the inside of the building to her, and they drove to the church and went inside and found everything as he'd envisioned it.

These stories do seem incredible, but remember that people used to think near-death experiences were crazy, too. But as more people opened up and started talking about leaving their bodies and what they had experienced, eventually there were enough stories from reliable people that these stories were accepted, published and shared publicly.

The idea that transplanted organs carry memories doesn't seem so farfetched, either, if you remember that your feelings, thoughts and beliefs are part of your chemistry. Every experience affects what is happening in your body and changes your internal chemistry. All your cells carry components capable of sensing your body chemistry and storing memory. When you don't feel well or are doing work you don't like to do, you are changed inside by the experience. When you love your work or when you have experiences of faith, hope and peace, those are reflected in your internal chemistry, too. Think of how you feel when you love what you are doing and lose track of time. These experiences and feelings become a part of your memories.

If you are changed physically by your life experiences, it is easy to imagine that doing work you don't like to do increases your chances of developing ulcers, having high blood pressure or having a heart attack. We know that experiences do affect the body because studies show that if you haven't made love with your spouse in the last year and nobody has touched you and held you, your odds of having a heart attack increase. If you do have a heart attack, your chances of recovery relate to whether you feel depressed and are alone or have a spouse who loves you.

When you repress feelings, you bury them in your body. You may succeed in forgetting unpleasant feelings and memories and putting them out of your conscious mind, but they don't leave your body. They are stored inside where they silently weaken your immune system. If you keep a journal, write poems and stories, and work at being aware of your feelings, your body does not have to store your pain, and you increase your immunity to illness.

When you do get sick, your body is asking you to become aware of what is stored within you. If you choose to ignore the meaning of your illness, if you choose to keep your feelings buried within you, you become a graveyard for your painful feelings, and they can kill you. This is the message Jesus delivered in the passage I mentioned earlier from the gospel of St. Thomas: "If you bring forth what is within you, what you brought forth will save you. If you do not bring forth what is within you, what you do not bring forth will destroy you." Remember, when you lose your car keys, it does not mean that God wants you to walk home. If you lose your health, look for it as you would your keys. Illness can be a messenger. It is not a punishment.

What memories or feelings have you erased from your mind but stored within your body? What is within you that needs to be brought forth? These are difficult questions to answer. To discover what you have stored within you, spend time dreaming, drawing, visualizing, meditating and praying. There are many books and tapes that can guide you. If you are not already spending time every day taking the lid off and releasing buried feelings, begin today. If you won't do it for enlightenment, do it for the health of it. Once you let your body and mind know you are open and want to heal, it will happen.

ix

Accept, Retreat and Surrender

How to start healing yourself

IF YOU VIEW ILLNESS AS AN OPPORTUNITY, then when you get sick, you can ask yourself, "Okay, what can I learn from this disease. What do I need to look at first?"

When I began working with Exceptional Cancer Patients I

noticed many of the group members lived longer than their doctors expected. I wanted to know why. I began to observe and inquire and noticed that the long-term survivors were the ones who began to pay attention to their feelings. As they expressed their emotions, made wise choices and became more spiritual, their bodies benefited. The physical changes were the side effects of an altered life.

Physicians call the most dramatic healings "spontaneous remissions." Once we have labeled them, we learn nothing from the people in whom those remissions take place. We cannot afford to ignore these remarkable successes. We are all at risk for a great many diseases, and as the world gets smaller the list of things we are exposed to grows larger. We need to learn from people who recover and people who stay healthy. In his novel *Cancer Ward*, Solzhenitsyn wrote of self-induced healing, which is a better term than "spontaneous remission." Solzhenitsyn chose a rainbow-colored butterfly to symbolize healing. The butterfly represents change and the rainbow represents all our feelings and emotions. We need to let the butterfly of change and emotional growth touch our lives if we are to heal.

One of the gloomy patients in *Cancer Ward* reacts to the talk of self-healing with this complaint: "I suppose for that you need to have a clear conscience." He is right. You do have to have a clear conscience. When you do the work necessary to clear your conscience, then the joy of living returns and the physiology of optimism restores you.

If you are ill or facing adversity, you can begin to heal yourself by following the paths others have followed. Forgive yourself and others, live with hope, faith and love and watch the results in your life and in the lives you touch. Remember that success and healing refer to what you do with your life, not to how long you avoid death.

. . .

What approach should you take to your illness? I have three words of advice: accept, retreat and surrender. Those three words might scare you if you were an inexperienced warrior going into battle, but others who have employed these tactics have won great victories.

You need to accept your situation if you want to be empowered to change it. I don't mean you need to accept any particular outcome of a disease, but you need to accept that the disease exists in your life and you are a participant. Once you accept that the disease or other misfortune has become a part of your life, you can marshal your forces to eliminate or alter it. If you avoid thinking about it, deny it or feel hopeless, you cannot play a part in changing it and your life.

Accepting the situation does not mean accepting someone else's prediction about what will happen to you. No one knows what your future will be. Do not accept that you must die in three weeks or six months because someone's statistics say you will. You are better off denying your illness completely than accepting a prediction that sounds like a death sentence. The best course, though, is accepting that you have problems while denying anyone's predictions about how your situation will turn out. Individuals are not statistics.

When I say "retreat," I don't mean withdrawing in the face of a more powerful opponent. For me a retreat means withdrawing to a quiet place where I can be aware of my thoughts and feelings. The quiet place may be anywhere; the source of true peace and quiet are inside me. In my retreat I withdraw from all the demands of life, but at the same time I am fully alive to myself and my loved ones. I do not always retreat alone. I can retreat with those who are close to me so that we can heal our forces and prepare to take on life when our retreat is over. When we return we are ready to fight for our lives. Bobbie and I regularly retreated when our five children were young. We needed the space and time to restore and heal ourselves.

When you have accepted, retreated and prepared yourself to fight, then you are ready to surrender. Again, you do not surrender to outcomes but to events. We waste so much energy fighting the nature of life. Accept the nature of life and surrender to it. When you do, you will have peace. When our energy is restored, we stop fighting things we cannot control, and we can start building our lives. Surrender is not about doing nothing; it is about doing the right things. When you surrender to the illness, you continue to receive your treatments, explore your feelings, repair your relationships and do all the other work of healing. But while you are working, you are saying, "Thy will be done" and not "My will be done." Surrender the pain, fear and worries and you'll be able to keep love, hope and joy in your life. As the Serenity Prayer tells us, leave it to God and rest.

> *Identify a challenge you faced recently: Did you face the adversity with a clear conscience? Did you accept your situation? Retreat to a quiet place to become aware of your thoughts and feelings? What does it mean to you to surrender to the nature of life or God's will? Now identify a challenge you are facing today: Is your conscience clear? What would it mean to accept, retreat and surrender?*

x
Animal Healing

How the experts go about healing

IN THE FIRST CHAPTER I SUGGESTED that you participate in groupet therapy and I admitted that Lassie is one of my role models. I am serious about how much one can learn from animals. This is especially true when you find yourself facing serious illnesses. Animals are the expert healers. I mean this in two senses. First, they exert a powerful healing effect on people through their presence and unconditional love. Second, animals often are able to heal themselves when they have life-threatening illnesses or injuries.

How do animals go about healing others? The first thing they do is accept their human companions without reservation. They pay no attention whatsoever to how you look or how much money you make or what race, religion, nationality or sex you are. Although they are not discriminating about what type of person you are, animals are very attuned to your needs. If you are sick, they sit quietly by you and provide their healing energy. If you need to exercise they try to get you moving. At the same time, they take their own needs and interests into account, but they do it in a subtle way that makes one laugh at their wisdom rather than get angry at their demands.

If you don't follow their prescriptions, animals forgive you and try to get you to understand why their suggestions are good for you. They never criticize. They just keep loving you until you love yourself enough to follow their directions.

When it comes to taking care of themselves, animals recover from diseases that overwhelm us. Why? Because they give and receive love so freely. When our pets are ill or injured, we are less likely to put them through all sorts of extreme treatments and more likely to bring them home and just love them—which often turns out to be all they need to recover. Remember the story of Oscar, the dog I was going to have put to sleep until our children intervened? We brought Oscar home and loved and nourished him, and in a few days he stood up and went out to play instead of dying of his melanoma. The vet was amazed and told us he'd never seen a dog that sick recover. I have heard many other stories about animals who were all but dead in the animal hospital and then went home where they were loved and where they recovered. As one veterinarian said to friends of ours about their cat, "Well, he was dead yesterday."

Lovers don't live forever, but they sure do exceed everyone's expectations and get a lot of enjoyment out of their time alive. Take a lesson from the animal world and be an expert lover: accept, love and forgive, and enjoy the life you create. We have seen it work in our family with people as well as with Oscar: Petting and loving are wonderfully effective medicines. If you don't have a pet, plants and trees are good teachers, too.

My prescription is a large dose of warm fur and a loving purr.

xi
Take a Siegel Kit with You

What to pack if you have to be hospitalized

I OFTEN SUGGEST TO PEOPLE that if they have to go to the hospital they take a Siegel Kit with them. The kit contains three things: a noisemaker, a Magic Marker and a water gun. The more I think about it, the more I realize we should always have a Siegel Kit handy. Every child should get one, with a set of instructions, when he or she enters kindergarten.

The noisemaker is for use in the hospital when you press your call button and the response is one hour of uninterrupted silence. Silence is good when you want to meditate. It is not good when you are calling for help. If you have a Siegel Kit with you, you can use the noisemaker to let people know you really need attention. This is important when you are not in the hospital, too. Our cat Penny is beside my chair crying for attention as I type this. She wants to be petted and will make a racket until I meet her needs. Every child should be as good as Penny at letting people know when he or she needs love and attention.

The Magic Marker is for use when you are to be anesthetized or sedated. You can leave a message for your surgeon like one woman did when she was having breast surgery: "Not this one, stupid." When they read your message, everyone is reminded you are a person, not a disease, and they treat you accordingly. Outside the hospital, the marker can be used on your body or on the refrigerator to leave notes for those who care about you.

The water gun is for use when you are not being treated with respect. I read about a nineteen-year-old dying in the hospital who used a water gun when people didn't respect his need for solitude. The water gun was his nondestructive way of expressing his anger at what was happening to him. The staff understood and allowed him the privilege of shooting them. When he died, the gun was passed on from the young man's mother to her son's intern and from him to an eight-year-old who had just learned he had cancer.

If every child had a water gun and was free to use it to say, "I am angry when I am not cared for," then parents, teachers, employers and others would be more careful and children would grow up healthier. When they can express their anger nondestructively, they do not have to store it within, where it can explode as rage and resentment. Perhaps some of the postal worker tragedies, mail bombings, school shootings and other sickening acts of violence would have been averted if water guns had been available to everyone or if someone had just listened to the person in pain.

Penny didn't need a noisemaker or a water gun to express

her needs. She just kept crying until I stopped my typing and cared for her. She did not hesitate to tell me what she needed because she knows that living things come before machines. Penny teaches us all to have a greater reverence for living beings and that it is all right to cry when we want attention. Don't get angry at those who make noise. Stop what you are doing and pay attention to the crying child, the howling dog and your wounded brothers and sisters. When we all learn these lessons, we will be as contented as cats wherever we go. Meanwhile, pack yourself a Siegel Kit for life's journey.

xii
Afflictions Can Be Fun

Why false hope is an oxymoron, and how to hold your life together

AN OXYMORON IS A COMBINATION OF WORDS that is inconsistent or incongruous. "Cruel kindness" is the example given in the dictionary. My two least favorite oxymorons are "false hope" and "detached concern." What does it mean to have false hope? How would you display detached concern? Neither makes much sense, yet some people in the medical profession use these oxymorons to criticize the message I deliver about love, peace and healing.

Think about detached concern. Young doctors are taught this so they do not become emotional. How do you show someone you care in a detached manner? What will the other person think if you are detached and do not show any emotions? Surely they will assume you don't care about them. Is that the price we have to pay to keep a safe distance from people with whom we work? Why? Try showing detached concern the next time you have a family problem.

I understand the need to make rational decisions that are not based on emotionalism, but it is possible to care for someone and not be hysterical when a crisis arises. We do it all the time in real life. I have operated on loved ones. I could care deeply about them and at the same time make the proper decisions.

Detached concern creates problems because detachment and concern come from the head. A better alternative is "rational caring." Unlike concern, caring comes from the heart. I am concerned intellectually about the things I read about but I care in my heart for people and I do what I can to help, without becoming irrational. If I feel my emotions may become so intense that they will cloud my judgment, I seek help. I can assure you that when I look for help, I don't look for a professional who will show me detached concern. I want a real person helping me. I often feel from my personal experience that my car dealer *cares* more for me and my car, while my surgeon *deals* with me and my diagnosis.

Why do I call "false hope" an oxymoron? Here we have to look at statistics. Can anyone really predict the future for an individual? Are individual outcomes determined by statistics? The answer is no. Hope is not based on statistics, either. Hope is a reality for the individual. I hope to win the lottery. I hope to get well. I hope to live longer than the doctor predicted. I hope things turn out all right. I hope for many things, and no one can say with certainty whether they will come to pass. We live in a world where the future is unknown, possibilities exist and miracles happen. In such a world, who can say that anyone else's hopes are false?

Bryce Courtenay's book *The Power of One* comes close to the point, even though it uses the term "false hope." One prisoner is asked why he gives false hope to the other prisoners. He answers, "Because false hope is better than no hope at all."

What some people object to when they talk about false hope is lying to patients and not telling them the truth about their condition. I don't do that. I tell people exactly what they are facing, to the best of my knowledge. But when family or physicians do lie to patients, the hope that comes from the lie is still a real hope. If the patient discovers the lie the result may be disastrous, but as long as the lie is unexposed the patient's life is much more pleasant and hopeful. As long as that hope is not preventing the patient from getting the best treatment available and doing the work of healing, the prospects are brighter where there is hope—even when it is based on a lie. Optimists, we know, live longer, healthier lives than pessimists—even when the pessimists have a more accurate assessment of the situation. That is why many alternative therapies work and even charlatans cure people. They give hope, and we call it the placebo effect.

How can you be truthful and still help people facing adversity and a bleak future? You can tell them they have sixty thousand miles left instead of trying to tell them the day or week they are going to die. When someone's doctor tells her she has six months to live, you can tell her to ask if the doctor will take a large bet against her living longer than six months. If someone you love is told he has a one-in-three chance of surviving his illness, you can send him to a statistician who will point out that statistics describe what happens to large numbers of people, not to individuals. The statistician will explain that numbers fall along bell-shaped curves that show one person may live a month and another with the same condition may live five years. You absolutely cannot tell from a chart where any individual will fall on the curve. As long as you are alive, there is always uncertainty. You can give hope and teach survival behavior in the face of uncertainty. No one will ever criticize you and say, "You gave me hope, made me laugh, taught me to love and I died anyway."

I have seen examples of the oxymoron that appears in the dictionary: "Cruel kindness" describes the behavior of some medical professionals I know. When I heard the phrase "laborious idleness," some family members came quickly to mind. But I don't ever expect to see a "jumbo shrimp" or a "legal brief," and I know I'll never see a "false hope."

A woman sent me a wonderful poem titled, "If Bilateral Mastectomies Can't Be Fun Why Have Them?" It plays on words like flat-busted and boob tube, describes the loss of a job opportunity at Hooters, how she made a clean breast of things and was glad to get that off her chest. The poem came in the mail with a photograph of Mr. Clean and the bald-headed poetess, and a note to me that read, "Separated at Birth."

The poem and the photograph left me smiling. That woman knows about survival behavior. I get many poems and letters containing healthy humor that grows out of the author's affliction. These wise people are seeing life in its fullest and not making the affliction the central point of their existence. Laughter can always remove fear and anxiety, no matter what the situation. You can't suffer when you are laughing. The two just can't be experienced together. It has to be one or the other, and joy always overcomes fear. Love creates, but laughter is the cement that holds our lives together.

People who rejoice in their afflictions are great teachers and healers. I have met many of them, learned from them and admired them. Some have afflictions that are not curable: quadriplegia, cerebral palsy, cancer, AIDS, loss of limbs, blindness. I could fill the page with dreary-sounding diagnoses—

and for each entry I could tell you someone who rejoices in the illness. One young man with Down's syndrome was asked to define "retarded." He said he meets people who see he is different and who can't communicate with him and are unable to get their "love flow" going. "They're retarded," he said.

These are the people we should learn from and emulate: the young man with Down's syndrome, the quadriplegic who paints with a brush in his mouth and the abused child who turned from suicidal thoughts, discovered the importance of love and went on to help others to find love. There are a lot of Helen Kellers in the world.

Some of these exceptional people have shared their stories. Tony Johnson's book about abuse, AIDS and love is called *A Rock and a Hard Place*. Max Cleland, a triple amputee injured by a hand grenade, is now a United States Senator from Georgia. He wrote *Strong at the Broken Places*. Sue Ann Easely, a woman with athetoid cerebral palsy and cancer, typed 250 pages with her nose. She had herself gagged and tied to control her drooling and movement while she wrote *The Bird with the Broken Wing*.

I can tell you they do not want you to compare your problems to theirs to make yours seem small. Everyone has his or her own problems, and amputees and people with quadriplegia will tell you that we should not compare problems. That misses the point. We all have our own problems and we have a choice about how we respond to whatever difficulties life brings us, large or small.

The Talmud contains a line that expresses the situation better than anything else I have read: "He who rejoices in the afflictions which are brought upon the self, brings salvation to the world."

Think about what the Talmud says about affliction. Now think about your own personal history. Do you know anyone who has learned to rejoice in his or her afflictions? How about

you? What afflictions have been brought upon you? Pick out
your most serious affliction: How would your life be different
if you were able to rejoice in that affliction?

xiii
This Too Shall Pass

Show your wounds and remember
these words

TRUE HEALERS REVEAL THEIR WOUNDS and show their limp. I
learned the benefit of showing my wounds when I shaved my
head in August of 1977 and saw how the hospital staff and
patients responded. It was not stylish to have a shaved head
then, and my sudden baldness signified to everyone that I was
a troubled man—which I was.

The day I showed up for work with a shaved head, patients
began to share their wounds with me. Almost immediately hospital staff—people I had known for years—told me things about
themselves that they had never revealed to me before. They knew
it was safe to speak to me because they saw my wound and figured I might offer them help from the wisdom of my experience.

We can all see the obvious wounds—the external scars and
deformities that show us you have sustained some traumatic
injury. But what of your internal scars—the wounds of the heart
and hidden parts of your life and body? People with external
wounds can help one another because they see in one another
someone who can understand their pain. They have traveled
the same path and can show one another the way to healing.
They are natives, not tourists, and can guide one another.

We are all wounded by life. We cannot exist without wounds and pain. They help define us and bring us together. People form survival groups to share their pain. They do not form groups to share their good fortune. Lottery winners seek out other lottery winners only when they realize the wounds that money can inflict.

You will be happier and healthier if you do not hide your wounds, external or internal. Join a group and help others survive by sharing your hard-earned wisdom. Remember that when you dress the wounds of others, you heal yourself. And remember to reveal your wounds. You don't necessarily have to shave your head, but if you want to be a healer you should at least buy a cane and limp.

There is a Hebrew prayer that says, "Thank you for giving us life, sustaining us and helping us to reach this day." I say that prayer each morning as part of my meditation. Psalm 118 expresses a similar sentiment: "This is the day which the Lord has made; let us rejoice and be glad in it."

How many of us get up in the morning feeling truly grateful for the day? Most of us wish we could turn the clock back and keep sleeping. The truth is, when you are happy to wake up and are grateful for the day, your life does change.

Each new day is an opportunity to pray for your loved ones and to act in a loving manner toward them. I start out by saying my prayer of thanks and asking for guidance and help from all available resources. I find I am always grateful for the new day, no matter how hard it is or will be, because I know I am not yet ready for my days to end. After all, the alternative to waking up and facing another difficult day is death. For all I know, after death the unenlightened may be sent back to wake up to the glory of the new day and its opportunities.

I want to experience more days and the difficulties and

opportunities they will bring. I want the chance to test myself. Maybe this makes me a glutton for punishment, but if I can help one living thing get through the day and not hurt anyone else in the process, I go to sleep thankful for the time I have been given and eager to awaken to tomorrow.

Days when I encounter more trouble than usual, I remember two stories. One is about a king who wanted something to help him in times of trouble. The king asked his advisers for words he could engrave on a medal to carry with him at all times, words that would be helpful no matter what problems he encountered. The king's advisers were unable to come up with a single, all-purpose motto that satisfied him. One day a wise old man came to the castle and heard the advisers talking about the king's impossible demand. The old man asked to be taken to the king, and when he was shown into the throne room he knelt before the king and said simply, "This, too, shall pass." The king instantly saw the wisdom of the old man's words. He thanked him, had a medal struck with the wise words and carried it with him to the end of his days.

The second story is about a lady who was suffering greatly over having delivered a stillborn child. A doctor at the hospital was very understanding and kind to her. A few years later she took a trip to China. There she saw an engraved plaque on a garden wall. She asked what the writing said, and the interpreter told her, "Enjoy yourself; it is later than you think."

The woman sat in the garden thinking about those words and her grief. She decided to have another child, and thought of the kind doctor. That evening she wrote him a letter and told him of the plaque that had helped her start living again. She thanked the doctor for his kindness and told him that she thought he had looked weary and should think about the words she'd seen on the plaque.

The doctor said he was awake all night after he read that letter. The next morning he went into the office and told his staff he was taking three months off. He traveled through Europe, and when he got back he found that some of his patients didn't know he'd been away. Others had gotten sick while he was gone but recovered faster without him. The doctor's time off was a humbling experience that taught him that he was not as important as he thought and that everything didn't depend on him.

When he goes to meet God, that doctor will not be surprised at the second plaque over Her desk. Remember I said earlier that She has three plaques over Her desk? You recall the first one says, "Everything you remember I forget and everything you forget I remember." The second plaque will be a comfort to everyone like the doctor who thinks he is important and who is worn out from trying to take care of everyone and everything. The second plaque says: "Don't feel totally, personally, irrevocably, eternally responsible for everything; that's my job."

You will encounter troubles every day. When the problems seem overwhelming, remember the lessons these two stories teach: Everything will pass. It is later than you think. And when you need a break, take time off and let someone else take care of the problems.

xiv
Our Primary Tools

Why we have been given a body, complete with problems

WITH ALL THE PROBLEMS OUR BODIES HAVE AND CAUSE, you might not think having one is such a great idea. Think of all the concerns, problems, repair work, expenses and limitations that go into living in and taking care of a body. When you think how much they add to our problems, you might ask why we have bodies at all. Angels and spirits get along fine without them. They don't have aches and pains. They don't need surgery, dental work or orthodontics. Why would our Creator give us something as troublesome as a body? Probably not just to create jobs for doctors, hairdressers and clothing salesmen.

Much as we complain about our bodies, they do give us the opportunity to manifest ourselves physically and make changes in the world. We have been given the opportunity to play the part of assistant creator, and for that work we need tools—and our bodies are our primary tools. Everyone's body is different; we have different physical limitations and abilities, but we all have areas of expertise where we can be assistant creators. When we accept our bodies and use them they become gifts. When we resent them or hate them they become burdens. Then they are more likely to manifest disease and teach us some lessons.

The question of whether your body is a burden or a welcome tool comes back to the question you answered in the first chapter of this book: What are you here for? If you have decided you are here to create, serve and provide, you will be grateful for the opportunity your body provides, no matter what its limitations. If you have decided you are here to use, be served and get what you can, you will find your body always leaves a lot to be desired and a lot to complain about.

In your next life you can decide whether you want a body or you just want to remain a free spirit. Remember, however, disembodied spirits can't taste, feel, paint or sculpt, fix plumbing or prune trees. I'll take my body, problems and all.

xv

The Last Problem You'll Ever Have in This Life

How to be prepared for the end of your life

WHEN I FIRST HEARD THE TERM "angel of death" I was confused. I had always thought of angels as helpers and guides, and the word "angel" had entirely pleasant connotations. Death and angels seemed incongruous. Angels are something I want around on a daily basis, but death is not something I wanted to experience any time soon.

It was hard to imagine how an angel of death could be angelic—until I learned that the word "angel" means messenger. The idea of a messenger of death made me stop and think. I would not like that messenger to show up today and announce it was time for me to meet my death, but I wouldn't mind if a messenger appeared daily just to remind me of my mortality. Maybe if a messenger of death visited every day I would lighten up a little and stop being so serious about everything. Maybe the messenger could follow me through the day and poke me now and then so I'd be more careful about what I put into my body and how I used my time. What an angelic gift it is to remind someone of his mortality.

Awareness of our mortality is a gift that enables us to live better. But the death that awaits us at the end of our lives may not seem like such a gift. For many people, dying is the biggest and most frightening problem in life. The truth is, death is not a problem. Your feelings and thoughts about death are the problem, and you can prepare yourself for a good death by the way you live.

As a physician, I've seen how people deal with the discovery that they are mortal. When they are diagnosed with life-threatening illnesses, the first thing some people want is a second chance. Before their illness they may not have been living with any conscious regret or actively searching for a better life. As soon as they are diagnosed, they want to seize missed opportunities, make better decisions and avoid disaster. When made aware of their mortality, they realize they haven't lived their lives authentically and the one thing they want is to be able to begin again. But life doesn't work that way. You can't live it in reverse. What is in your rearview mirror is history.

In the wonderful movie *Harold and Maude*, Ruth Gordon plays an aging woman who is well aware of her mortality and has a zest for life. "Reach out. Take a chance. Get hurt, even," she tells a young man who is more attracted to death than to life. Maude doesn't need a second chance because she has lived her first chance. You can, too. Or you can put off living and hope you will discover your mortality through an illness that gives you the permission you need to live. You won't get to start over from the beginning, but you may have enough life left to begin living for the first time.

Perhaps you believe there is an afterlife and an opportunity to come back and make up for our mistakes and learn the lessons we were meant to learn. I won't argue with you. I may even agree, but that doesn't change my feeling about what I want to do with this life. I don't want to rely on an afterlife to make up for what I missed in this one. I want to live fully and learn enough in this life so that when they ask me if I want to come back for another life, I can say, "No thanks. I need a rest, not another chance to learn."

6
Surviving Good Times

i
Oh God, Why Me?

The dangers of good health and good fortune

WHEN YOU LEARN YOU ARE MORTAL, you get very wise, very quickly, about what to do with your limited lifetime. But what happens when you stay healthy and don't get a wake-up call? When your life is going smoothly, what is there to motivate you to look at questions like why you are here and what do you want to do with the time you have left?

Don't get upset if you are healthy and don't have a lot of problems. You can learn from other people's adversity. My father's father died when my dad was ten years old. When I was a boy, I heard my dad say that losing his father was one of the best things that ever happened to him. That loss influenced everything my father went on to learn about life, people, money and survival. "I learned that we are here to make life easier for each other," he said. His life was a success because he did make life easier for his family and all those who needed him. I listened and observed and learned from him, and now I hope his story will make life easier for you.

You don't have to experience sickness or loss to discover your mortality and be grateful for life. It is no coincidence that God had Adam and Eve eat from the tree of knowledge and not the tree of life. He wanted them to learn they were mortal. You can learn from them and many others who have come before you. Do not wait for a disaster to strike. Calling 911 when you are in a spiritual crisis doesn't work. If you cry out to God, She will hear you. But why wait until your soul is living in darkness to open communications?

The light and the darkness are one—just as good fortune can be bad, so-called bad luck can be good. Remember God's directions and the universe's schedule. There are times in my life when a so-called problem turns out to be a gift. All that is required is that I not judge the event, but be open to possibilities.

Life is like a school. We are here to learn and be educated. There are many levels of enlightenment in life, just as there are many grades in school. In the school of life, it is perfectly all right to audit classes and learn from the experiences of others. If you do, you will be promoted to a higher grade the easy way and be ready when graduation day comes. On that day you will receive a kiss on the cheek from our Creator, and be reunited with Her.

I am not afraid to play the lottery regularly because I am prepared to win. After I win and am asked how I feel about winning, I plan to say, "Oh God, why me?"

Why respond that way? Because winning the lottery is dangerous to your health and well-being. Most lottery winners say, five years later, that winning ruined their lives. I have had people in my office telling me how their lives were ruined by vast sums of money. As soon as they had great wealth, they felt pressure to be impossibly successful all the time. Of course, that's absurd—they could have given the money to charity if they didn't know how to live with it. Or they could have given it away to someone whose life they wanted to ruin. I know a lot of people who would have been happy to help them with their problem. That is one of the dangers of wealth: You get attached to it and can't give it up even if it is making you miserable. You find yourself working for a lord you can't have faith in or enjoy relating to.

Do you still envy lottery winners? Before you answer, let me tell you the story of four men who won millions of dollars. The men went to a Las Vegas casino together and made a pact to share equally all their winnings or losses. The first night, one of the men hit the jackpot. He won millions and brought the money up to the room so they could all sit around and have fun looking at it. After a while, they became hungry. Two of them went out to eat and bring back food for the two who stayed to watch over the money.

The two guarding the money got to talking about how long their newfound fortune would last. They calculated how much longer it would last if they didn't divide it four ways, and decided to kill the other two when they returned. Meanwhile, the two who went out to get dinner were doing some calculating themselves, and also decided it would be a shame to split the money four ways. So they poisoned the dinners they were bringing back for the other two.

When the two men returned with food, the ones guarding the money let them in and lured them into the bedroom, where they shot and killed them. While they waited for nightfall to dispose of the bodies, they recounted the money and started dividing it up. Since they were hungry, as they finished counting the money, they ate the dinners the dead men had brought back. The next morning the housekeeper found four dead men and their money. Before she called the authorities she flushed the money down the toilet so it wouldn't cause any more grief.

Remember earlier in the book when I talked about the man who robbed our hotel room? I said events are not the problem—our thoughts or feelings about events are the problem. The same is true of good fortune. Wealth by itself is not a problem, but if you have great wealth your feelings about it can cause you great problems. Knowing what people can be like, the cleaning woman was wise to get rid of the money. Let us hope that some-day we can all find happiness without needing to win the lottery, but that if we do, we will know how to handle it.

Your attitude determines whether tough times turn out to be beneficial or whether good times will make you miserable. The third plaque over God's desk is a reminder of how much our attitudes affect our lives. It says: "If you go around saying, 'I've got a miserable life,' I'll show you what miserable really is, and if you go around saying, 'I've got a wonderful life,' I'll show you what wonderful really is. [Signed] God."

> Remember the other two plaques I told you God keeps above Her desk: "Everything you forget I remember, and everything you remember I forget." And: "Don't feel totally, personally, irrevo-cably, eternally responsible for everything; that's my job."
>
> Perhaps God could use some new enlightening plaques that I haven't seen. Given what you think about God, what other plaque or plaques would you like to see placed above Her desk? I'd like to see "God loves you" or "I love you just the way you are."

ii

Death and Peace

How you can rest in peace your entire life

I HAVE CHANGED MY POLICY about dead animals. When I was jogging, I used to clear all the dead animals off the road. I'd hold a little prayer service for each animal as I moved the body from the pavement and laid it on the earth. I still collect the cans and bottles I see along the roadside but I don't remove the dead bodies anymore. I did not stop moving them because my wife was worried that I'd bring some home dread disease or get poison ivy. I changed my policy because I decided it is important that we stop denying death and hiding it from view.

We have scores of ways to say someone died without using the word "dead." You know the euphemisms: "He passed away, failed, bought the farm, is resting in peace, kicked the bucket, left us, went to heaven." Every family has its own favorites.

I now leave dead animals in the road where they are visible and I avoid euphemisms because I want us all to be aware of death so we think more seriously about life. The dying people I've worked with have taught me what a great teacher death is, and I also have experienced death's lessons in my life. Twice I have had accidents that could have killed me: once as a child when I choked on a toy, and once as an adult when I fell off our roof and hit my head on the pavement. Those two experiences remind me that death is a reality. I accept that I will die, sooner or later, and I can live more fully because I accept it.

Who or what can give you peace? Nothing but your own mind. You must live peace to experience peace. If your peace of mind depends on the world meeting your needs, you won't find peace very often. When you do, it won't last. Would it bring you peace of mind if the kids were quiet for a while, the bills were paid, the roof stopped leaking and time passed more quickly or more slowly? Maybe, but all the things you would like rarely happen at the same time. More often, life presents you with difficulties. A lasting peace will never come until you change your mind about what you need, and learn the difference between what you want and need.

When you die, someone will likely stand over your body and say, "Rest in peace." But you don't have to wait until you are dead to rest in peace. You can have peace while you live. True peace comes when you have faith. That peace depends not on external events but on the state of your mind. You are the source and the recipient. If you have faith, you will R.I.P. the rest of your lifetime.

> *What do you need to have peace of mind? Think of all the things that rob you of peace of mind and all the things that could provide you with it. Are your lists full of things that depend on the actions of other people? If you decide your peace of mind depends on others, then you have two choices: You can accept that you will not have peace of mind very often, or you can decide to create peace within yourself by altering your life.*

iii
How Did I Get Here and May I Go Now?

Thinking about God before disaster strikes

GOOD HEALTH AND GOOD FORTUNE can lull you away from doing the work necessary for personal and spiritual growth. When you are comfortable, you may be able to forget that you are going to die. You may start thinking it is safe to base your peace of mind on your health, the behavior of others or your luck with the lottery. You may even find yourself thinking that you don't need God. After all, you have those three new lords: your money, a healthy body and prestige.

I once heard a man say he knew there was a God, he just didn't think he needed Him. It is nice to take care of yourself and be independent, but it is also nice to know that you have a resource to rely on in times of need. If you are used to fending entirely for yourself, then when a catastrophe occurs you will expend a lot of energy looking for help at a time when you need your energy for creative work.

When you realize what is available to you, you spend less time being a victim. The rules are very simple: When you have the energy and motivation, you handle whatever comes your way. When it is too much for you, say a prayer, leave it to God, and don't judge what God decides to do. The best thing to pray for is God's help in becoming like a god, in the sense that you develop the ability to handle all that comes your way. If you want some direction, look to God—He's a great role model and coach. With the strength obtained through prayer, you can do God's work.

. . .

I took a class in enlightenment. For the final exam, the teacher gave everyone a chicken and said, "Take your chicken home tonight and kill it where nobody can see you. At our next class tell me how and where you did it."

At the next class, I still had my chicken. The other students laughed at me. When class began, they were all anxious to speak. One after another they stood up and told the teacher where they had killed their chickens: In the basement. In the garage. In the bathroom with the lights out. In the woods behind the house. Finally I was left with my squawking chicken. I said "I could not find a spot where I couldn't be seen. I could not go anywhere where there wasn't a presence. God is everywhere." I received an A on my final exam.

If you live with God's omnipresence in mind, you'll live a very different life.

I didn't ask to come here, or did I? Who decided I should be born at this time and place? If I'm not making the decisions, I may have some problems. If I'm not in charge of my schedule, I may have trouble leaving when I want to.

I've had a pretty interesting life, so it is easy for me to think someone else is directing the show. I have a sense there is a greater plan and we are all part of it. Things may happen or not happen for reasons we can't understand. When one person dies in an accident or by disease and another doesn't, I don't think it says anything about the value of the individuals, but I do think it is part of a plan. One person may survive because there is work left for him or her to do. Maybe survivors are left here to inspire others to do some important work, or to learn or teach certain lessons.

When you accept that you are not in charge of everything, you can begin to work with the one who really is in charge. That has been my experience; when I accepted that I was not in charge and started to work with someone else's plan, the Boss showed up. Now we are a team and I have less to be concerned about. He organizes my schedule. I just follow it, and when He is taking a day off my wife steps in.

iv
Before Adversity Strikes

Things to do when you are healthy and comfortable

GOOD TIMES CAN BE RISKY, but you can turn them to your advantage. Here are some things you can do before disaster strikes. Think of them as survival behaviors to help you get through good times:

Say yes to drugs.

Prepare for hot spots.

Wear life loosely.

Clean house.

Marry yourself.

Prepare for heaven.

Find happiness.

Give yourself a day of rest.

Don't be confused by the list. I will explain how these behaviors can help, but first I want to caution you against filling up your life with too many responsibilities. You know what it feels like to spend a day being busy. You have lots to do, time is short, you are under pressure. Hurry up, get to the next task, check your list, did you forget anything? There is traffic, red lights and your next stop is across town. As you plow through your list of responsibilities, you feel the energy of life draining out of you. You begin to wonder, Why am I doing this? Is this what my life is about? Maybe in my next life I will only have to worry about lighting a fire, building a shelter and catching my next meal.

We are encouraged from an early age to keep ourselves busy and productive and out of trouble. But the truth is, being busy isn't necessarily healthy and it doesn't keep you out of trouble—especially if you stay busy so you have no time to be aware of your feelings. Your body stores those unacknowledged feelings, and you know that is not good for you.

I don't want to spend my life keeping busy. Maybe I could successfully juggle an impressive list of responsibilities, but what would I be contributing to life? I am much more interested in being creative than in being busy. Creating feels good. It fills me, restores me, nourishes me and energizes me.

There are many ways to be creative. You can take scrap wood and build your cats a series of shelves, boxes and mazes. You can write, paint, shop or talk to people. When you are creating, you will feel the sense of creation in your body, and time will not exist. If you have forgotten what a sense of creation is, go look at a baby. When we see a baby, we see potential. Remember that we are all former babies and we all have the potential within us. Go to the nearest mirror and reflect on it.

v
Marry Yourself, Prepare for Heaven and Find Happiness

How the survival list can help you get through good times

Here are some ways you can work at fulfilling your potential while you are still healthy.

Say yes to drugs. The other day I attended a conference on the choices available to individuals interested in exploring healthy lifestyles. Hundreds of booths displayed healthy products to support a variety of lifestyles. I suggested to the business owners that when they returned home they should hang signs in their store windows saying, "Drugs Are Good for You. Take Them."

They looked a bit puzzled until I explained that nutritious food, herbs, supplements, vitamins, love, prayer and exercise all affect the chemistry of our bodies, just as surely as drugs do. Yes, I am using the word "drugs" in a broad context, but why not think this way? It might help us to remember that everything we put into our bodies gets metabolized. Most everything having to do with our bodies, thoughts and feelings also changes our chemistry, for better or worse. So why not practice saying yes to the drugs that help the body stay healthy and fit?

I regularly say yes to the drugs that bathe my body when I exercise, express love, pray, am massaged, meditate or take vitamins and supplements. I can feel their effect, and I know they are helping me to be a vibrant and vital human being. When you start thinking about your worth and you build your self-esteem and self-love, you activate healthy chemistry within your body. You can produce a healthy high that can never be matched by any artificial means. The original producer has all the patents, and they cannot be improved. It is a true near-life experience.

Prepare for hot spots. You've probably seen pictures of people walking barefoot on hot coals. Fire-walkers can walk for a hundred feet on burning coals and not get burned. Most of us would be safer crossing hot coals if we put shoes on first. What is the point of barefoot fire-walking? It is an exercise in choosing carefully where you are going and protecting and empowering yourself.

If the entire world is a hot spot, does it make more sense to wrap the world in shoe leather or put on your shoes? Putting on your shoes is a lot simpler.

Be aware of your path and the hot spots that lie ahead. To prepare for what lies ahead, you must get in touch with the mystery of life. This is not a logical or intellectual exercise. If all your decisions are based on logic, the path you choose will be path-o-logical and you will get burned.

If you are to participate in the work of the gods, and the God, you must pay attention to the feelings created by the paths you choose. If you do, you will have a wisdom that comes not from classrooms but from the gods. Then the next time someone places hot coals in your path, you will be prepared to walk on them—or to put on fireproof footwear if you are not yet ready to walk barefoot.

Never mind what others think of your choices. How does your path feel? Move forward when the time feels right. Listen to your heart, not your watch. Your watch cannot tell you when the time is right. Its beat is constant and does not vary according to the heat of the situation. Your heartbeat does vary; listen to it.

Wear life loosely. If you see life as a loose garment, you will have an easier time living. Think of life as something you drape around yourself but are not firmly attached to. Let it be something you can slip out of easily, at any moment. Living this way will help you focus on the important things in life and let go of the insignificant details.

If you are more concerned with your life than with your appearance, you will have the time to live more fully. Remember, time is the essence of life. How do you want to spend your time? Getting dressed or wrapping yourself loosely in a comfortable garment and getting involved in the life around you? I don't want to waste time every day dressing myself so I can impress the world. I want to be free to move and live and enjoy life and not be confined by other people's expectations. Make sure you have a comfortable fit when you dress for life. Take your tie off, loosen your belt and wear sneakers.

Clean house and find a storage place for your memories. I am not suggesting that you write your autobiography so your family will have a record of your memories. This exercise has nothing to do with what you consciously remember. I am talking about the life experiences that you have stored in dark places.

You know what your basement looks like. When will you get around to dealing with the memories stored there? When will you clean out your basement so you will have more living room?

Your body is your dwelling place. You store your life's memories and experiences in every cell. Remember the stories about transplant recipients whose new organs bring along surprising details about the donor's life: everything from the donor's wife's name to a description of the donor's murderer.

The fact that we store our memories in our bodies like we store old furniture in the basement should inspire us to start cleaning house. If you leave the painful old memories piled in the basement, you can damage your residence. Clean house now, while your dwelling place is still sound—then enjoy the living space and time you create.

Marry yourself. Masculine and feminine qualities are a component of both sexes. Men and women need a balance of masculine and feminine qualities to remain healthy and respond properly to life. A man, for his survival, needs to be comfortable with relationships and able to express emotions. A woman in the business world will need certain masculine qualities to survive and be recognized. This is not about power and control or being the patriarch or matriarch, but about being a complete human being who can respond appropriately to life's difficulties.

Being strong and never crying can kill you. That is not being masculine; it is being stupid. Being a mother is not being feminine, it is role playing and it is dangerous; when the kids leave home, Mother quickly becomes no one and has no reason to live.

Be someone and be sure that the someone you become is capable of being assertive and direct, as well as sensitive and caring. Since married couples have the best survival statistics, why not be one? Let your masculine and feminine natures marry each other.

Prepare for heaven. My belief is that we are all headed for the same place when we die. Some of us will call it heaven and others will call it hell. How can one place seem so different to different people? The things you do in this life determine whether you will have a joyous or hellish experience when you get there.

If all your desires are focused on things you want for yourself and you are not trying to help other living beings, you are headed in the wrong direction. No one can acquire everything he desires. If you live a life of self-interest, you cause yourself pain and suffering. If you live by a code that says do unto others what you don't want done unto you, you are hell-bent.

Since we all end up in the same place, think of the greeting you will get when you arrive. The people you did a disservice to in life will all be there to meet you. Some who come along after you will remember you, too. How will the people you have known in life speak to you and about you? Will they have any kind words for you? What do you think they are going to say to the condominium owner and board? If your life has been guided by self-interest, you will find yourself in unpleasant surroundings, and it will feel like hell. Excuses and explanations won't help.

If you want an eternity of joy, use this life to provide for the happiness of others, within your means and in your own way. When you are working for the good of all of God's creatures, you will find happiness in this life and the next. When you pray not for personal desires but for God's will and the world's benefit, then you are headed for first-class accommodations.

When you arrive at the final destination there will be a large group waiting to greet you and show you to your beautiful condo with a view. If you have ever been on a vacation where you were surrounded by the beauty, peace and harmony of nature, you already have a glimpse of what awaits you. You will unpack, get settled and then walk out on the balcony, look around and say, "This is heaven," and you'll be right.

Find happiness. I was on an airplane the other day and a flight attendant said, "We're not happy until you're not happy." At first I didn't connect the two negatives and thought he was saying the attendants weren't happy until the passengers were. When I realized he was saying they wouldn't be happy until they made someone else unhappy, I asked what it was all about.

He explained, "One of the airlines is having a labor dispute and that's the employees' motto: 'We're not happy until you're not happy.' They want the CEO and executives to feel badly about the way the employees have been treated."

What a sad way to get enjoyment out of life: making someone else unhappy so you can be happy. Getting even never really brings satisfaction. I see what malpractice suits and revenge can do, and they don't restore your life even if they are successful in punishing the person who hurt you. I am not saying that legal action is never indicated, but even when you win a case, does it put your mind at ease? I think you may gain more by telling the person who hurt you, without accusing or blaming anyone, how you have suffered. You may or may not get the other person to understand what he has done to you, but if you share your pain with him and he changes because of it and does not injure someone else, then you have accomplished something.

Suppose a bird flies into your window and breaks its wing. You can end its misery and give it a nice burial in your backyard, or you can bring it into the house, restore it and then release it when its wing has healed. Which choice will bring you more joy? How do you feel as you watch it fly away? Do you need it to call, send a card or visit to say thank you?

Emily Dickinson said:

If I can stop one heart from breaking,
I shall not live in vain;
If I can ease one life the aching,
Or cool one pain,
Or help one fainting robin
Unto his nest again,
I shall not live in vain.

You find happiness in life not through getting even, but through helping others. At your funeral, wouldn't you rather have people remember you for the aching you eased than for how often you got even or made others unhappy? I know the difference it makes from my dad's funeral. The number of people who appeared to thank us for his help amazed us.

Give yourself a day of rest. I've said many times that God wants us to be aware of our mortality so we will use our time wisely. The Sabbath speaks of the same thing. God rested on the seventh day and told us to set it aside as a holy day so we could rest. He asked us to celebrate the day and to use it wisely. It is hard for me to believe that the Creator really needed a rest, with His unlimited resources. I think the rest day was created for us, to make us think about what we are doing with our lifetime.

I don't think we have to sit and do nothing on the Sabbath, but we shouldn't be working. Think of how the word "work" makes you feel. "I have to go to work." That is not a sentence most people enjoy saying. If we are working on the Sabbath we are sinning and wasting our time, but if we are contributing to life and creation,then we are using the day properly. The seventh day is for rest and re-creating, and for being as aware of our time as God wants us to be.

> *Here is an exercise you can do when you feel you have lost your sense of direction: Stop and take the time to see where your life is headed. To find out where you are heading, take this test. Most often, do you find yourself taking the time to do what you want to do or taking the time to do what you don't want to do? Your answer will tell you where you have been spending your life.*
>
> *Now ask yourself: Where is my present path taking me? Am I willing to go there? Do the things you are taking time to do fulfill your heart's desire? Remember that you don't have*

all the time in the world to decide. You only have your lifetime,
and the future is unconsciously prepared long in advance. So
get to work now.

vi

An Expensive Education

Sometimes it is wiser to follow in the footsteps of others

MOST OF US LEARN THROUGH OUR DIFFICULTIES and mistakes, but that is a costly way to learn. We suffer while we learn, and the people around us suffer, too. As a young physician, I assisted others until I learned how to do various procedures. Then I was allowed to do them under supervision. And finally when I had the expertise, I did them on my own and then taught them to others. In life, we tend not to follow such a sensible training system. Too often we are unwilling to listen to experienced elders, or have no mentors from whom to learn. Instead we set out to show everyone what we can do on our own and end up needing help to get out of trouble.

There is no doubt you can learn by getting lost; personal experience is a great teacher. I have learned much from my inadequacies, egotism, immaturity, ignorance and pain, and the problems I cause myself and the people around me. But learning through mistakes can be an expensive way to get educated. The tuition cost is very high. I would rather have a capable teacher show me the way, whenever possible. It is less painful and expensive in all ways.

No matter what you do, however, life will bring you new

experiences and along with these experiences, new problems. You'll need to practice your skills for dealing with and learning from problems since you won't always have a teacher or guide to follow. But when you have a choice, it is foolish to ignore a path laid out by others who have passed this way before you. No matter how capable or talented you are, a coach or guide can help you develop your abilities.

I thought about paths one winter morning after a blizzard. I went jogging through a cemetery where no one had been since the storm, and each step was difficult because the snow was quite deep. The second day after the storm my run was much easier because I could follow my own footsteps. A few days later because of the cold weather, the snow had turned to ice and it was dangerous to try to run in my own footsteps. The storm reminded me that there are times when following a well-trod path makes life a lot easier. At other times it is wiser to find a new path. There are many guides in life who can show you the way through difficulties, but when their ways do not fit with your life, then it is time to strike out on your own. Be sure to choose your path honestly and wisely. Your goal is not to impress your peers or prove something to anyone else. You are the only one you need to impress and be comfortable with.

Stop now to see whether the tuition costs you are paying are worth the education you are getting in Life 101. The key is remembering that you should be learning new skills, as well as gaining new knowledge that truly educates you. It is wise to be aware that difficulties lie ahead on your path, but just knowing that is not enough. You need to learn how to deal with those difficulties—only then will you be educated and prepared for life's obstacles.

Remember that a good teacher does more than inform you. A good teacher educates you, increases your self-esteem and leaves you prepared for life. If you find a guru or teacher who does not do this for you, leave and find another who can help you uncover the wisdom within you.

vii
Hands, Heads and Heart

How to decide where to go and what to do

I WAS GETTING ON AN ELEVATOR when I noticed a man coming down the hall limping and using a cane. He looked like he had had a stroke, and I held the elevator door open for him. I thought to myself, If he had a broken heart I wouldn't have known it and might not have been so inclined to help.

Our wounds have the power to change other people. When we share our afflictions openly, we let others know they can speak to us about their own difficulties. The world is changed by the wounded. They have the passion to do anything, from raising funds to restoring compassion to the world. The problem is that broken hearts aren't visible. I know from experience that every one of us is wounded, but most of us hide our wounds and don't see them as the gifts they are. If you buy a cane and use it tomorrow, you will change the people you meet and they will treat you differently. You will become the privileged listener to tales of woe told by the people you meet. They will reveal the wounds inside and begin their healing process.

Just as a knife can drain an abscess and start the physical process of healing, a wounded listener can help drain the pain of an emotional wound and help the healing process begin. As the angel in Thornton Wilder's story said, "In love's service only the wounded can soldier." Expose your wounds and begin to heal yourself and others.

You have been given hands with which to work. Hands with which to care for yourselves and others. But where do your hands get their directions? Do the directions come from your head or your heart?

If you listen to people trying to decide what to do with their lives, you can tell when they are deciding with their heads. It doesn't feel good to listen to them. Their reasons for doing what they are planning to do don't ring true. When people rely entirely on their intellect, they forget how to feel and they go on and on rationalizing their decisions. When people make decisions from the heart, they speak with a vitality and energy that can be felt even over the telephone. They are alive and they know how to use their hands to do what needs to be done in the world.

I am not suggesting that you decapitate yourself or be empty-headed, but that you live in your heart. Then your work will be creative and you will be fulfilled. If you listen to your heart, it will talk to you not only of your own needs; it will direct you to do what is right for you and for the world. The heart knows and lives by a code that heals us all.

There is a reason we don't have songs advising us to follow our heads. The lyricists are right: Follow your heart, and you will get where you are meant to go and do what you are meant to do.

viii
Being, Nonbeing and Bumble Being

Finding and fulfilling your true obligations

YOU CAN BE IN PERFECT HEALTH and still discover your true path. You can become enlightened even if burdened by great riches. But it takes more work, largely because we rarely find enlightenment unless we are looking for it.

I live the lessons in this book. I have a quiet time every day when I listen to the voice. I use my meditations and the prescriptions in this book to help keep me from losing my way. The Kabbalah tells us to take the time to hear the voice. The voice is available to us all. When you find peace and quiet you will hear the voice. When you live in fear and chaos you will hear only the voices of those around you. It is not just silence that is the key, but a life with a rhythm that allows you to hear the voice.

There is light and dark, full and empty, existence and nonexistence, being and nonbeing. In other words, there are living, conscious beings carrying out activities. There is also lifeless matter, without consciousness, that may function but not by its own choice. I call the latter "nonbeing." When we are meditating or in a trance we come close to a state of nonbeing, but we never quite reach nonbeing. We can sit like a nonbeing stone, but we still have being because we have consciousness. When our bodies die, our consciousness can live on, and we then experience nonbeing in a different way. But since upon death we lose the ability to alter matter directly, we also lose the ability to perform acts in the world. We are in a state of nonbeing, from the standpoint of life and creation.

We need our minds and bodies to live and be creative. With a mind and a body, you have the ability to act in the world and be a co-creator. The problem is that it is all too easy to go astray. Much of what we do to ourselves and to the people we touch is destructive, not constructive. Sometimes we make a mess of the job of being and reach a third state of existence I call "bumble being." You can avoid bumble being by living your life fully and consciously by choosing the path of creativity and having the correct lord as your foreman.

The idea of obligations makes some people uncomfortable. You may feel limited or burdened by the idea that there are things you are expected to do in life. But try to look at obligations differently. What is it you feel obligated to do with your life? What are you here to accomplish? What is required of us? Once you answer those questions honestly, your life will have direction and you will be creative. You will not spend time doing what others think you should do. Obligations are enlightening when you realize your only real obligations are to yourself. Obligations are a burden only when you are obligated to the wrong things. When you are obligated to the true task of your life, all else falls into place and you are free to live.

Set aside time today to be quiet and aware of the rhythm of your life. Think about what you are trying to accomplish. What is guiding you? What voices direct you through the day? Are they taking you where you believe you were meant to go?

Think about your obligations. Are they a burden, or are they guiding you along your true path? Ask yourself again, "What am I here for?" Only you know the answer. You know it in your heart. Unlock your treasure chest. Don't be satisfied with just knowing what you are here for. Go out and live it, today. All you really need is heart.

7
Prescriptions for Living

i

False Advertising

Finding the power you need to make changes

"INFORMATION IS POWER," the radio announcer said. I don't remember what he was selling but I remember thinking that he had a lot to learn.

Information is not power. It does not change anyone. The people with the most information about problems are often not the ones working hardest to solve them. It is the people affected by them who are motivated to change things. Think about it: Who raises funds to cure diseases and help the needy? Who works to fight pollution and clean up our planet?

Every guidebook for life should come with the label: "Batteries Not Included." No matter how many guidebooks you read or how many coaches or mentors you have, no one can provide the energy you need to change your life. If you want to make changes, you need more than information and more than a guidebook or a mentor. You need power.

Power comes from inspiration. Inspired people get things

done. When we are inspired, we grow, change and develop new abilities. We make ourselves into better people and help create a better world. Inspired people knock on doors, walk miles, comfort others, start organizations and do whatever it takes to get things done. I ran my first marathon to raise funds to fight leukemia. Why? Because the father of a child with leukemia asked for my help. You will find the power to do what needs doing when you are inspired by something greater than yourself. This chapter has prescriptions that can bring you closer to the one thing that can inspire you and give you the power to change yourself and the world.

ii
Gratitude: Why and for What?

What you can and should be grateful for
every day

WHEN I GO OUT JOGGING in the morning, I sometimes notice how much the weather influences people's response to life and to one another. When it is gray and rainy, many people look unhappy. When the sun is out and the temperature and humidity are comfortable, people are smiling and calling out to one another, "Hello, isn't it a lovely day." For me, a lovely day is any day I wake up. If I'm awake, I'm grateful to be alive and to have another day to experience life.

I speak as a realist, not an optimist. I know that the longer I live, the more problems I will have. So what is there to be grateful for? I am grateful every day for the opportunity to have more problems, to learn how to live with them and rejoice in them. That is enough, but there is more to be thankful for. Every day is another opportunity to love and interact with God's creation, and on some days to be a cocreator.

The weather or the events of the day do not determine whether I am grateful for my life on that day. Every time I jog through the world, I am awed by what I find. On a winter morning, when it seems too cold and slippery for safe jogging or bicycling, I can still go out and experience the glory of sunlight turning icy branches into strings of sparkling diamonds. The day a dog bites my butt as I jog by a house with an open gate, I am grateful for learning that a dog bite isn't as bad as I feared it was. I'm also grateful for the payment I'll get from the dog owner's insurance company, which I plan to give to our granddaughter. After all, I was bitter while visiting her.

If your gratitude depends on what life gives you or what other people do for you or to you, you will be disappointed more often that you are grateful. But you can learn to feel grateful by rethinking your attitude toward life. First, remember that contentment lies in giving. If you know that giving is better than receiving, then you can feel grateful for what you are able to give others. This does not mean you ignore your own needs. You will decide what to give and how to give it, and then at the end of the day you will be grateful for having had the chance to give in your own way. Remember, we all have something to give, and our ability to give is not related to our finances or physical strength.

Second, be grateful simply for being alive. When you are grateful for life, pure and simple, your life becomes one you can be grateful for. That may strike you as circular or even backward logic, but your attitude really does have an effect on how things work out. When you can't change your life any other way, you can still change your attitude. When you do, your life changes. You find more chances to love, and you will be surprised to see how much more love is returned to you.

The next time someone says, "It's a lovely day," try saying, "Yes, it is." Today is always the best day of your life. And that is why this book is dedicated to life. Painful, wonderful, life. Crazy human comedy.

I mentioned earlier that writing and painting can teach you to see things through the eyes of an extraterrestrial. Try this exercise in the morning to make yourself aware of the beauty of the day and all the things you might be grateful for. When you wake up, look at the world as if you had arrived on this planet during the night and this day is your first chance to look at the Earth. You will see flowers, colors and a whole host of things you may be so used to that you are blind to them.

If you use your extraterrestrial eyes all day, you will find that no matter how difficult the practical aspects of your life, this planet is still a very special creation.

iii
Watch What You Put in Your Mouth

Choose between spreading dis-ease and promoting healing

WE ARE ALWAYS TELLING OUR CHILDREN to be careful about what they put in their mouths. We are careful not to buy small toys they could choke on. If we see a child pick something up from the ground and put it in her mouth, we take it away and scold her. And of course we are careful about what we put in our own mouths.

How many of us have the same concern with what comes out of our mouths and our children's mouths? Over the course of our lifetimes, we do more harm with what comes out of our mouths than with what we put in. Interestingly, the what goes in and the what comes out of our mouths are intimately related.

If you teach your children to have a reverence for life, they will have a reverential attitude toward all living beings, themselves included. They will think about what they put in their mouths because they will want to nourish their bodies. They will also be conscious of the need to nourish their spirits. In taking care of themselves, they will become aware of the needs of others. With their mouths and bodies, they will try to nourish and sustain other living beings.

What comes out of our mouths originates at a deep level of our being. When we are healthy at this deep level, we spread wellness by our words, smiles, looks and attitudes. Our love of life is expressed by every part of our bodies. If you pay attention to what comes out of your mouth, you will quickly learn about what is inside you. If you are not healthy inside, then what comes out of your mouth and body will be sick, too. When your words are sick, there is disease inside you; you may not see physical signs of disease yet, but it is there and it will eventually manifest itself. What you eliminate and excrete will tell you a good deal about yourself and your inner state of health. And what comes out of your body, especially your mouth, has a profound effect on others.

Watch what you swallow and what you accept into your mind and what you take to heart. Everything we ingest affects our own health and the public health when the stuff comes back out. You can spread toxins and dis-ease or you can promote healing—it all depends on whether you are ingesting (and eliminating) toxins or therapeutic agents. What did you ingest in the past twenty-four hours and can you digest it in a healthy way? More to come on that subject.

You know what nourishes and what destroys you. What did you accept into your mind, incorporate into your body and take into your heart in the past twenty-four hours?

What came out of your mouth in the last twenty-four hours? Did you speak healing words? Were you short-tempered? Were your words angry or unpleasant or impatient? If you spoke words of dis-ease, look inside yourself for their source.

iv

To Err Is Human, to Forgive Is Feline

Strive to be feline

I AM CONTINUALLY AMAZED at our pets' capacities for forgiveness. I constantly complain and remind my wife about the terrible things she does, such as leaving the bathroom lights on. She reminds me that I eat too fast. Meanwhile, our cats forgive us both for these and all our other horrible flaws.

If I step on one of our cat's tails, she doesn't attack me. She doesn't remind me how many times I've done the same stupid thing. She doesn't ask, "Why can't you watch where you're going?" or yell, "Watch out. Here he comes again." The cats don't like it when I brush their teeth and comb knots out of their fur, but later that night they will sit on my lap as I watch television and rest on my chest when I go to bed, purring loudly to let me know they love me despite what I've done to them.

Why are they so forgiving and easy to live with, while people are so difficult? I think it is because they are born knowing something we have to discover. They know who they are and why they are here. Do you know why life was bestowed upon you? When you answer that question correctly, your life will change and you will become more loving, accepting and forgiving of yourself and others.

I look across the room at my feline teachers and I am grateful for their teachings and love. They remind me to ask the right questions. I know the answers whenever I remember to ask the questions. I know what I am here to do. Now I have to go and practice my purring, get my back scratched and my tummy rubbed.

> *I prescribed forgiveness earlier, but this is so important that I'm giving you a refill. Take a few minutes to think about forgiveness. Is there anything anyone has done that you cannot forgive? If you find yourself unable to forgive someone, go back and ask the key questions again: Why are you here? What do you need to understand? Why was life bestowed upon you? When you find the right answers to those questions, you will be almost feline in your capacity to forgive. Now you have two role models, a cat and an earthworm (more about that later). Things are looking up.*

v

You, Me and Nature

Stop and listen

NATURE IS OUR GREAT TEACHER and friend. I fear, however, we take it for granted, as we often do our true friends. It is hard to appreciate how much our lives depend on a blade of grass, an insect, or a worm we may never see. They are all part of the plan of creation. They all interact to provide us with a place we can call home: mother earth. When we destroy parts of nature, we interfere with the plan of creation. Interfere enough and we will destroy our planet and our home.

I understand you sometimes need an exterminator to eliminate termites, ants or bees from your home, but these insects are just doing what they were created to do. But, in general, I am talking about the bigger picture. The papers and television newscasts are full of reports of floods, earthquakes, hurricanes, forest fires and other catastrophes that warn us we are intruding in places we do not belong. Our very survival is related to where we choose to erect our buildings, what we put in the air, what we do to the water and forests. Our consciousness and actions affect our planet.

In a newspaper the other day, a college student was asked whether he was concerned about the lumber industry clearing forests and destroying the habitat of owls. The student knew about the issue but didn't see a dilemma. His frightening answer was "It's only an owl."

What comes next? It's only a tree, beach, dog, tiger, person of another race, religion, nationality. It's only a _____. You fill in the blank. You tell me which part of God's creation is dispensable.

If we think we are separate from nature and other beings, we are on the path of self-destruction. We have been given the freedom to think and act for ourselves, but what about those around us and those who come after us? We are not really separate from them. We must learn to think not in the you-and-I mode but in the we mode. We must think of future generations and what we will leave them. No matter what your past has been, you can choose to care about all living beings. The next time you toss a can from your car or leave trash on the beach, think what you are saying about the future of life on our planet.

A long time ago the Bible warned us about ourselves. After God created each thing, He looked and saw "that it was good." But on the sixth day, after He created man, God did not look upon this creation and say, "It is good." I think God realized that the big picture was a good one, but man was a potential problem. God knew free will to be a dangerous but vitally magnificent and meaningful thing.

Let's show our Creator His trust was not misplaced when He made us and gave us freedom of thought and action. Let's be developers of the planet, giving consideration to all forms of life. Let's never single out any form of life and say, "It's only a _____." We were made in the image of God. That statement is not about our good looks, but about our actions.

The next time you have a free moment go for a walk in nature and observe it closely. Lie on the ground and look at what surrounds you. Listen to the wind, the waves and the animals. You will not find anything dispensable. You will find everything in creation calling to you, alerting you to the path you must follow.

When I go for a walk in nature, I listen. As I type this I can hear the birds outside my window chirping and singing. If you want to hear the voice of creation, take the time to be by yourself in your special place and listen. Quiet your mind and all will be made clear to you by the voice that speaks to you.

You do not need to walk in nature to hear the voice. The key is finding your place away from the distracting sounds that normally surround you. When you find your rhythm, you can hear the celestial voice, whether you are sitting in a room alone, exercising or even driving your car. How will you know if it is the true voice? Listen to what it is telling you. You will know when the voice speaks of creation, love, faith, hope, peace, revelation and enlightenment.

> *If you can't tell the difference between a robin singing and the clatter of civilization, find a quiet place for yourself and turn on your hearing aid. Listen right now. What do you hear? I hope you hear the words of the one who wrote the song for the robin to sing. As the spiritual tells us, "Somebody bigger than you and I."*

vi
A Role Model for Troubled Times

Consider the skunk cabbage

A ROAD I JOG ON REGULARLY was repaved recently. In the weeks that followed, I noticed a place where the new asphalt rose up several inches, cracked and finally opened like a small volcano. What came belching forth, though, was not lava but a plant. The sight impressed me so much that I brought the family out for one of nature's free therapy sessions.

When everyone was gathered around and I pointed out the amazing sight, Bobbie said, "Honey, it's only a skunk cabbage." I said, "Only a skunk cabbage? Look at what it has done! Look at what it is telling us!"

If you were a seed and someone paved over you, how would you know which way was up? What would you do if a wall was placed before you? Or what would you do if you were a bacterium newly confronted by antibiotics? Survival mechanisms dwell within us.

A seed contains an incredible intelligence that knows which way to grow. It senses gravity and doesn't even need the warmth of the sun to tell it which way is up. It doesn't let statistics kill it, either. What were the odds that a paved-over skunk cabbage seed would ever see the light of day again?

Remember that seed when you run into difficulties. The seed knows what it is and what it will become and how to go about growing. Each cell in your body is as wise as a skunk cabbage seed. Each cell has the information and intelligence it needs to perform its daily activities, even in the face of adversity.

Take a look in the mirror and admire yourself. You are a wonder of creation, no less than a skunk cabbage. The next time a wall appears to be blocking your way, take your inspiration from the skunk cabbage seed and keep growing ahead until you create an opening through which you can burst forth to grow, bloom and blossom.

A skunk cabbage is not the only teacher you'll find in nature. All of nature offers lessons on living, free of charge. One morning I noticed a dead tree supporting many living things—fungus, vines, lichen—which taught me that even after death we can continue to support those who live on. Living trees on our property teach other lessons. One tree has grown around a barbed wire fence. Another has grown around a nail, and a third through a chain link fence. These trees teach me how to accept irritation, absorb the pain and grow around problems. Nature teaches me how to find my place, grow toward the sunlight and bypass obstacles. To survive, we must be able to change in response to whatever is required by the challenge of the moment. Our bodies know this, but our minds often rebel when change is necessary and they choose death over the challenge of life. Your true desires, intentions and determinations are made known to your body. You are the germinating seed.

*What is the major problem in your life right now? Identify it
and then walk out into nature and seek an answer. Ask nature
how to solve your problem. I guarantee that if you observe and
listen, you will receive an answer. Nature always has the
answers to your current problems and timeless reminders of
the big lesson: We are here to be compassionate to all living
things. We survive challenges and change when we support one
another and devote our lives to one another.*

*Be grateful for the wonderful therapist whose rates are so
reasonable. The only payment you need to make comes from
your heart. Don't be late with that payment. If you are, the
Creator may institute a rather severe late payment penalty:
You may lose it all. So be grateful for the questions and go out
and find your answers before the light goes out.*

vii
Who Did That, and Why?

Consider the earthworm, a worthwhile role model

I HAVE BEEN THINKING recently how much there is to admire
about the earthworm, an incredible creature that finds almost
everything organic edible. We are elevated spiritual beings,
made in the likeness of God, but if we ate what the earthworm
eats, we would die of food poisoning or starvation. That, however, is not the most impressive thing about this incredible
creature. The really amazing thing happens after the earthworm eats toxins: It digests them and then eliminates a non-
toxic waste material that serves as fertilizer. Now that is holy

shit. The earthworm can save life as we know it on our planet if we don't overwhelm it or destroy it with our environmental abuses.

The earthworm spends its life caring for the planet, and we can't even be bothered with throwing our garbage into a receptacle. If the earthworm could eat glass, plastic and metals, we wouldn't have to clean up after ourselves, but there is a limit even to the earthworm's abilities. It is time we stopped talking about our spirits, souls and the afterlife, and started living here on this planet with the earthworm as our model.

If I ever start a business or become part of a team, I will make the earthworm our mascot. Our motto: "We can swallow and digest anything you throw at us, turn it into fertilizer and make it a growth experience."

Now the other side of the coin, something that impresses everyone. Think about the beautiful fall foliage in the New England states. Why does nature perform this color-changing trick? God's original thought was to increase tourism and help the New England states' economy. I pointed out to God that there is a more significant, symbolic reason. I think the changing seasons and brilliant colors are metaphors for our own nature and lives.

The colors that appear in the fall are there all along in the leaves, but they are covered up by the green. When autumn arrives and the leaves shed their green, their true colors show forth. The green leaves are pleasant to the eye in their own way, and they can remind us of life's opportunities, but they are not awe-inspiring like the autumn colors. Crowds of people do not head for New England in the spring to admire all the green leaves.

We spend much of our lives as green leaves on the family tree. While we are green, we fit in, do not attract attention, do not disturb anyone and are hardly noticed. But each of us has brilliant colors hidden within. When the autumn of life comes, it empowers us to show our beauty and individuality before we let go of the tree of life.

I want you to ask, "Who did that?" the next time you see something beautiful. When you see a work of art, stop and reflect on the Creator. Go look at a flower, a beautiful painting or look in the mirror, and ask yourself, "Who did that?" If you are aware of the precious works of art around you, you will take better care of them and of yourself. The artist went to a lot of trouble to create what you see, so don't destroy what has been done. A thousand-year-old tree deserves to be looked at in awe. A tiny wildflower rising out of the earth, a baby elephant, each creation is a work of art. Ask who is the artist, so you can get to know Her and take lessons. And remember that you are part of the artwork you see.

viii
Watch What You Plant

Facts are not what we need

IT DOESN'T MATTER HOW MUCH YOU FERTILIZE your garden, nothing will grow if you plant stones. I have nothing against stones. They are very quiet and soulful and don't cause problems unless someone picks one up and throws it at you. Stones are independent and detached. They make beautiful walls, but the walls only separate people and do nothing to bring them together. Stones are like sterile facts: Left to themselves, they accomplish nothing. If you plant stones, your garden will remain sterile and unproductive.

Living seeds, like living thoughts, grow and produce life. A living seed seeks the light and rises through all kinds of obstructions to burst forth into the world. Seeds have the amazing ability to sprout through a crack in the sidewalk or to lift, split and push aside pavement to find the light of day. A vital, living thought is like a seed in that it can move whatever lies in front of it, expose itself and change the world into a more beautiful place.

Science may be interested in learning how the seed knows which way is up, but understanding the seed's gravity-sensing mechanisms is less important than appreciating the way it changes the world as it grows. Thoughts also change the world. Facts don't change the world or us—unless they inspire awe in us. Then we are changed but it is not the fact that caused the change; it is the feeling about the fact.

Seeds and thoughts germinate and grow and change us and the world. We need to focus our concern on the seeds of the world, whether they are acorns or ideas or children. We need to help all growing things reach their full and unique potential. Put your compost where it will do the most good.

Today we teach our children (and ourselves) how to use things to get answers. We don't really care if they comprehend what they are doing. For example, I use a computer and I have very little idea what makes it work. We no longer revere the things we use. We have become more concerned with facts and numbers and have little time for awe, understanding and wonder. It is sad to grow up in a world where people are interested primarily in knowing how to do things. The same attitude infects nations and drives them to seek the power and knowledge to do things so they can threaten other nations when they do not get their way.

Let's hope that someday we will spend more time teaching ourselves and our children to revere things. An astronomer said that when we look at distant stars, we are seeing events that took place thirteen billion years ago and that we will be busy for the next thirteen billion years figuring it out. Think of that. The light we see now in the night sky has been traveling toward us for thirteen billion years! That fact should inspire in us a sense of awe. Try to imagine how far light travels in thirteen billion years. Imagine how big the universe is to contain stars thirteen billion light-years away from each other!

It is overwhelming to consider. And yet, though the facts we learn about the universe may be interesting and even awesome, our lives should not be centered around collecting facts. We are here to feel, wonder and gaze in awe at the world. Instead of just teaching our children how to use things and do things, I suggest we nourish their sense of wonder.

Think of yourself as a landscape artist. Plant seeds. Plant thoughts. Plant yourself. Care for your garden in a way that will produce the healthiest, most beautiful plants. Don't forget that one of the plants in the garden you are tending is you.

We can all create ourselves. We can grow, bloom and blossom in response to our own tender care. Our pains are the compost and our tears are the water that softens the soil and helps us spread our roots and withstand the winds of fortune.

As you work in your garden, you will hear a voice asking, "Who are you?" and "Where are you?" Prepare now for that voice. Ask yourself, "Do I have an answer for those questions? Do I know what I am creating?" If not, step back and look at the seeds you have planted. What is growing in your garden? What do you see reflected in the pond in the center of your garden when you look into its still waters?

ix
The Tree of Life and the Family of Man

What to do in a perplexing situation

As YOU TRY TO FIND YOUR AUTHENTIC PATH in life, remember that nature presents us with many symbols and messages. We can learn from nature because we are part of nature, and the lessons we see there really do apply to us, too. We are leaves on the tree of life. We perform necessary functions so the tree flourishes and grows while it nourishes and supports us. We are part of the cycle of life, just as we are part of the tree of life and it is part of us. There are many trees but only one family and one garden in which we all grow.

We learn from nature that there is a cycle of life and that winter comes for each of us. We will be replaced by new generations. I see the new growth when I look at our grandchildren. They are the seeds that will give rise to new trees with new leaves. When the winter of our lives arrives, we will fall from the tree and provide for those who follow by enriching the soil from which they will grow.

More important, we can each experience our full potential and uniqueness in all the seasons of our lives. Each of us is free to create and none of us needs to be afraid to fail. If we become our unique selves and display our true colors and patterns out of love, we have nothing to fear because what we do can only turn out right. We go wrong only when we act out of fear and concern for what others will think of us.

We need to learn to be excited by our beauty, not by our sins and tragedies. We need headlines and pictures in the news that show the beauty and not the horrors, but this will not happen until we make such beautiful pictures that they cannot be denied their proper place.

We are all here to serve in our own unique ways and to give back to the earth and to life what we have been given. We are here to contribute the one thing that makes us immortal: love. We cannot hold on to the tree of life forever and we cannot live forever through our actions. But if we act out of love, the sacrifices we perform will sustain those who come after us, and our garden will have many beautiful trees. When we each make the choice to serve, no one will suffer because of someone else's desires. No tree will go without nourishment or be cut down to fulfill someone else's wants. Our garden will flourish because each seed will have rich soil and each leaf will be free to display its beautiful colors for all to see. It will be an awesome garden that will make the front page of every newspaper.

> *Only you know what you need to do to live a happy life. You are the expert and know the secret lies in loving, forgiving, believing, accepting and creating. You probably intend to do all of that, and are deciding now when you are going to start living your authentic life. Stop deciding, just do it!*
>
> *Remember this: Now is the only time you have. When God created the universe, it was now. You can't say to creation and energy, "I'll do it later, not now." Later doesn't exist. Creation doesn't know anything but now. Whenever you get around to doing what you want to do, it will be now. The things you need to do to live a happier, more fulfilling life—the only time you can possibly start doing them is now.*

We have a prayer bowl at home that gives off beautiful tones when it is rubbed or struck. When you are struck by one of life's happenings, do you ring true? We could all ring true like that if we listened to the wisdom of the sages—and if we acted on what we heard. Remember that the information others provide will not change you. You must supply the energy. You must take the time to restore yourself and to create. Choose the right prescriptions and make them a part of your daily life. Listen to the voice, follow your heart and live an authentic life. Then when you find yourself in a perplexing situation you will no longer need a role model. You are now one of the sages. You can ask yourself, "What should I do now?"

My Favorite Recipe

I want to leave all who read this book with a gift of my favorite recipe for Life Pudding. You deserve a reward for your courage, determination and inspiration.

First, set the time aside to prepare your life pudding without interruption.

Then, take a liberal helping of love and stir in enough compassion and commitment to create the desired consistency. Season liberally with humor and blend the ingredients until they meet your taste. Set aside to rise to the occasion while you prepare the icing. When it is firm enough, place it in the form you desire.

Mix action, wisdom, devotion, prayer and chocolate syrup in a large container. Layer it thickly over your life pudding, whatever form it may take, making sure to cover all the corners.

Ask your grandparents to look it over and advise you about any changes in appearance or taste they believe are called for before you present it to anyone.

When you are satisfied with the result, garnish with reverence and devotion.

Let stand and season at room temperature until you feel it is ready to be served, and then serve generous portions liberally during your lifetime. Protect from extreme heat and cold. Remember that it is low fat and low calorie, and safe to consume in large quantities whenever you have a hunger for life.

The more you serve to others, the more fulfilled you will be. Do not hurry the process. Take the time to savor what you have created. If you do, you will find, as I have, that you will feel more full when you share your life pudding with others than when you consume it alone. Actually, I find I don't need to consume much, because serving others is what nourishes me.